"If you want easy answers[...] for you. But then, as Honeycutt points out, [...] might not be the religion for you, either. In place of explanations that 'airbrush the oddities' from the miracle stories, Honeycutt here challenges us to ponder anew how these odd stories continue 'happening in the lives of those who hear and heed them.' He enriches his challenge with sound biblical scholarship, pleasing word craft, and tales from a master homiletician."

—**Mel Bringle**, Brevard College

"The dead walking? Water into wine? How is a Christian in the twenty-first century, or for that matter a skeptic—how is *anyone* to make sense of the Bible's miracles? Might I suggest you start with Frank Honeycutt's remarkable *Miracles for Skeptics*? Wed a deep understanding of Scripture and faith to references that range from Harry Crews and John Updike to Barbara Taylor Brown and Austin Powers, add generosity, stir in wit, and you have something approaching the pleasures of this book. Funny, learned, and deeply moving, *Miracles for Skeptics* is theology for the rest of us. And that is high praise."

—**Mark Powell**, author of *Hurricane Season*

"In *Miracles for Skeptics*, it is Frank Honeycutt's willingness to acknowledge doubt that makes his message of faith all the more powerful. He is a gifted writer, and his words and wisdom are much needed in our troubled world."

—**Ron Rash**, Western Carolina University

"In his latest book, Frank Honeycutt revisits some of the most challenging events in the New Testament. Readers hoping to make peace with these hard-to-swallow stories, though, will find no easy answers, no logical explanations or pat interpretations tied neatly with a bow. Instead, knowing that the most powerful tales resist one-and-done interpretations while rewarding each new encounter with fresh insights, Honeycutt invites us to examine these paranormal occurrences through the lens of 'all the skepticism with which [we've] been blessed.' His rigorous hiking and cross-country cycling journeys provide an apt metaphor for the sojourn into Biblical events that defy logic and reason. Like the protagonist of his short story 'Virginal Laptop,' which serves as the penultimate chapter, Honeycutt discovers new meaning in these odd tales—revelations that, in the author's words, beckon us in 'unpredictable, risky, and life-shaping' new directions."

—**Nancy Lewis Tuten**, Columbia College

Miracles
FOR Skeptics

Encountering the
Paranormal Ministry of Jesus

FRANK G. HONEYCUTT

William B. Eerdmans Publishing Company
Grand Rapids, Michigan

Wm. B. Eerdmans Publishing Co.
4035 Park East Court SE, Grand Rapids, Michigan 49546
www.eerdmans.com

Book design by Lydia Hall

Printed in the United States of America

30 29 28 27 26 25 24   1 2 3 4 5 6 7

ISBN 978-0-8028-8315-5

Library of Congress Cataloging-in-Publication Data

A catalog record for this book is available from the Library
of Congress.

In memory of Andy Coone

1953–2020

Contents

CONTENTS

Acknowledgments

Many thanks to the kind folk who read chapter drafts, offered thoughtful ideas, and provided general encouragement as this book took shape: Larry Harley, John Gifford, Cindy Honeycutt, Mark Graham, Kent Oehm, Lukas Honeycutt, Paul Pingel, Nancy Tuten, Howard and Tina Pillot, Dan Shonka, Christa Compton, Michael Kohn, Chris Lawrence, Tom Ward, Barbie and Furball White, John Hoffmeyer, Gary Safrit, Josh Kestner, Rachel Connelly, Tony Metze, Pat Riddle, Ed Davis, Jon Heiliger, Doug Sullivan-Gonzalez, Wayne Kannaday, Chris Heavner, and Teddy Carfolite.

The Value of Skepticism
in the Christian Life

You desire truth in the inward being; therefore teach me wisdom in my secret heart.

—Psalm 51:6

I recall a Sunday afternoon in December of 1986, about ten days before Christmas in the Shenandoah Valley. My first parish, in the heart of Virginia's apple country, consisted of two small Lutheran congregations (Trinity and Saint Paul) in and near the small town of Stephens City. Several parishioners could trace their family roots in the valley to the mid-1700s. Massive orchards stretched all the way to the base of Great North Mountain, viewed from the front steps of one of the churches, now closed, built along a beautiful stretch of rural road known as Cedar Creek Grade. Just shy of thirty, I was definitely plagued with the youthful exuberance that accompanies most pastors only a year out of seminary who tend to look back on the previous week and feel they could have done more, said more, prayed more, and seen more church members struggling with a variety of pressing issues.

With the crunch of all the special holiday services looming on the near horizon, it felt good to collapse in the parsonage den on our tattered "This End Up" sofa with a beer and the fat weekend edition of the *Washington Post* and try not to think of the many people on our church prayer list who were facing one (or more) daily realities of the intercessory trio of illness, grief, or worry—the long roll of names we intoned just three hours ago in church (and every Sunday morning) before God the healer. Hannah, our first child, fifteen months old, slept peacefully down the hall in her crib. I was fully prepared to join her soon in Slumber Land there on the couch.

An essay in the lifestyle section of the paper, written by a young father named Brad, caught my eye. Its title was irresistible—"My Baby Is Very Sick: But I Can't Pray for Him."

There is perhaps nothing more agonizing than being a parent for a critically ill child. Time crawls. Appetite vanishes. Sleep evades. I've accompanied many families to the pediatric wards of various hospitals, and some of the same families to cemeteries after that. Words sometimes seem empty and pointless, offered into air. Caring friends (and compassionate pastors) might consider taking cues from Job's three pals who didn't try to explain the tragic events of previous days or offer empty words of comfort: "They sat with [Job] on the ground seven days and seven nights, and no one spoke a word to him, for they saw that his suffering was very great" (2:13). Like me at times, Job's friends eventually resort to chatty (and unhelpful) explanations, but at first they got it right.

No one spoke a word. I like that. Far too many inane Christian responses to tragic events float around emergency rooms and funeral homes. If you've ever tuned in to *The Righteous Gemstones* (HBO)—the rather over-the-top but sidesplittingly funny TV series about a South Carolina family and their twisted evangelical empire—

you know that creator Danny McBride and the writers of the show have experienced their share of silly and shallow theological bromides that somehow have staying power worthy of full lampooning.[1]

Noting that silent accompaniment is never wrong, in my own thirty-one-year pastoral ministry, I found that it usually seemed to help families like Brad's to hear, "I'm praying for you, daily."

"Everyone is praying for my son Alex," Brad wrote in the newspaper essay I was reading. "Everyone but me."

Alex was on a respirator tube. His upper esophagus ended at midchest. Left untreated, this two-day-old baby would starve. He needed an immediate operation and long days of treatment. I've reread this father's essay several times since that December Sunday afternoon. Decades later, his honesty still strikes me:

> Family in Maine prays, friends in Oregon pray, whole congregations in the District say "Lord, hear our prayer," when the priest announces Alex's name and condition. My wife's sister, a master of theological studies candidate at Virginia Theological Seminary, has mobilized the whole faculty and student body to petition God on my son's behalf. Certainly, I should join in. It seems reasonable, expected. My longtime alienation from organized religion is no excuse now—if there are no atheists in foxholes, one might expect

1. For an entertaining review of *The Righteous Gemstones*, see Doreen St. Felix, "Sinnermen," *New Yorker*, January 24, 2022, 72–73.

there are no lapsed Catholics in intensive-care nurs-
eries . . . the cold, metallic, foreboding machinery of
medicine pressing and piercing the warm, defense-
less body of a newborn, seems tailor-made to pull
a prayer from a tired father's soul. Only a monster
would fail. I lean against the wall again and look out
the window. I cannot do it.[2]

The psalm snippet (51:6) that opens this book was
penned by a man who calls out to God after an incident
that differs markedly from the context of a worried father in a pediatric ICU. Following a series of deceitful
and selfish royal decisions, King David asks God to create a clean and truthful heart via this honest request
offered several millennia prior to the anguish accompanying the illness of baby Alex. And yet this verse, part
of an old and famous prayer for renewal and change,
seems to fit this devoted and skeptical dad who cannot
pray at all. His reluctance and inability to pray is utterly
authentic, honest, and real. And he candidly questions
whether invoking God can make any difference in the
slightest during his son's agonizing balance between life
and death. If God indeed desires "truth in the inward being," a cessation of all theological games and pretending,
perhaps Brad—gazing tenderly with hope and through
tears upon his damaged son—is closer to authentic truth
in his own internal gut check than many Christians
who never question God's power at all.

2. Brad Lemley, "My Baby Is Very Sick: But I Can't Pray for
Him," *Washington Post*, December 14, 1986.

In Miriam Toews's wonderful novel, *A Complicated Kindness*, a teenager named Nomi grows up in a theologically rigid faith community in Canada where TV shows like *Bewitched* are forbidden because of the magic that might lead to Satanism. Nomi begins to question the consistency of this stance and loses respect for her pastor whom she sarcastically calls "The Mouth." (Note to self: If you really want to discover how sermons are coming across, poll a few teenagers.) Nomi recalls a conversation with her sister and a friend about banned sitcoms that might compromise the faith development of young people in their church because of supposed sorcery. "But you can take a stick and tap a bush with it so it bursts into flames? Yeah, and check this out, in my right hand I hold five fish. In my other, a single loaf of bread. Now watch closely as I. . . . My mom said hush."[3]

This is a book about the various "miracles" (a word rarely used in the New Testament; more on that later) of Jesus in the Gospels and his deeds of unusual power that attracted scores of disciples, curiosity seekers, and also enemies, even though Jesus consistently seemed to downplay their importance and tried (unsuccessfully) to keep them quiet. This is also a book primarily written for people like Brad and Nomi and many friends of mine who admire the teachings of Jesus but are pretty convinced that anyone who seriously ascribes to the weird stuff in the Bible is a couple steps away from admittance to a good psych ward.

3. Miriam Toews, *A Complicated Kindness* (Berkeley: Counterpoint, 2004), 16.

I've been blessed with an abundance of friends who've never quite understood why I became a pastor: people like my Maine homesteading friend Andy (whose friendship spanned forty years before his death a couple of autumns ago)—one of the most compassionate and gentle people I've ever known, his patience with and love for mentally challenged children knew no bounds—who once told me that he'd "chase God down with a pitchfork" if he ever met the Lord on the road one fine day; people like Larry, an attorney, my longtime pal and cross-country bicycle-trip companion (seventy-seven days across three major mountain ranges from Puget Sound to the coast of Maine along the northern tier of the nation), an occasional churchgoer who shuns any belief in divine metaphysicality and whimsically refers to himself as a Frisbeetarian ("someone," he says, "whose soul floats up on the roof like a Frisbee at death and you just can't get it down"); and people like Anthony, an organic-farmer friend who once asked, "What in the wide, happy hell are you doing with your life, Frank, bothering with these tall tales that most of us gave up decades ago along with Mother Goose?"

Perhaps you also cherish (and sympathize with) close friends like these. Perhaps you admire the teachings of Jesus but can't quite wrap your head around why his followers take seriously strange stories that seem better suited for *The Twilight Zone*. Perhaps you resemble a character in one of Lorrie Moore's short stories who perceives God (if you believe in God at all) as a rather removed deity who in the past occasionally "glanced up from his knitting, perhaps even [rose] from his freaking wicker rocker, and staggered at last to the window to look."[4] Perhaps you sit in a church pew on many Sundays and feel a bit embarrassed to consult your pastor with questions no one else seems to be asking. Perhaps you are pondering the possibility of baptism (for yourself or your child) but find the paranormal parts of the Bible a serious stumbling block to further consideration of life in a congregation of Christians.

This book is for each and all of you. I will not encourage you to shelve your doubts as you read these chapters. In fact, I hope you'll embrace them as literary interpretive allies in sleuthing out truth and meaning for tales that may (at first glance) seem as outlandish as the exploits of Paul Bunyan and Pecos Bill, characters you left behind many years ago with the tooth fairy.

The Bible's most famous skeptic, Saint Thomas, unfairly maligned by many through the centuries of Christian history, eventually arrives at the most mature theological confession about Jesus ("My Lord and my God") of any early disciple—*precisely through his doubts, not in spite of them*. There's also a powerful detail about his reservations about the resurrection that many miss. After expressing Easter skepticism to his friends, Thomas remains in the community that became the church for a full week (John 20:26), presumably continuing to voice his consternation and doubts. Far from judging this early skeptic, his friends welcomed Thomas's reservations in a very open-ended fashion that suggests even

4. Lorrie Moore, "Beautiful Grade," in *Collected Stories* (New York: Knopf, 2020), 52.

a lifetime of raising good questions if he needed such. Thomas, curiously, was also known by his nickname, "the Twin" (John 20:24). His identical sibling is never revealed in the Gospels, which may suggest a kinship with careful readers whose questions and skepticism are an important part of any path to truth.

I'll be delighted if someone reconsiders the church after reading these words. I am, after all, a pastor and do regularly confess a belief in "all that is, seen and unseen," as the Nicene Creed puts it. The rather bizarre creative existence of oddities such as giraffes, beluga whales, black holes, mitochondria, and the color magenta (all rather miraculous and difficult to explain, if you ask me) collectively embolden this pastor to consider just about any curious oddity the Bible throws my way, including (if you're wondering) a virgin teenager who gives birth in a barn to a unique baby.

However, conversion through coy cudgel and manipulation has always been a rather dark stain on certain eras of Christian history. In the pages to come, I'll attempt to offer (always incomplete) responses, not answers, to folk resembling my aforementioned excellent friends. But, first a promise: this book will not covertly attempt to convert wayward souls, or try to persuade anyone that certain mysterious stories—ranging from turning water into wine for happy wedding guests to engaging in ambulatory buoyancy on an open sea—really and truly happened with a then unknown Galilean who developed a reputation for pulling off the paranormal. Such an enterprise, in my pastoral experience, is about as compelling as searching for remaining remnants of the real Noah's ark.

There is lasting power in the miracle stories of Jesus but never a coercive power that seeks to overwhelm one's intellect, will, or doubts. God "cannot ravish," wrote C. S. Lewis. "He can only woo."[5]

Perhaps God is drawing you to Christ via the very stories you've heretofore found troubling and downright weird. This book is my open invitation to examine the miracles of Jesus—ancient narratives involving healing, wonders in nature, and even demonic encounters with unseen forces of darkness—with all the skepticism with which you've been blessed.

5. C. S. Lewis, *The Screwtape Letters* (New York: Bantam Books, 1982), 23.

1

The Breadth of the Miraculous in the Bible

Miracles are a retelling in small letters of the very same story which is written across the whole world in letters too large for some of us to see.

—C. S. Lewis

Homo sapiens are a tiny twig on an improbable branch of a contingent limb on a fortunate tree.

—Stephen Jay Gould

I love the Bible, even the weird parts—maybe *especially* its unusual stories—and read it aloud every morning before dawn (followed by a sometimes off-key hymn greeting the new day) with my wife, Cindy, who continues to recover from a stroke that affects her speech. Initially, she could not speak at all, a frightening reality for a bubbly and loquacious woman who taught high school English her entire career, a vocation centered upon words.

The Bible is a library of events first shared *orally* that occurred well before various writers took stylus to scroll, followed by centuries of debate that ultimately stitched the stories, letters, travails, and feats of faith into various books bound together in a single volume. It makes sense to regularly read this large and sometimes imposing bestseller aloud, pondering how the strange tales may have first sounded to incredulous ears and timid tongues like mine.

A bald prophet enlists a pair of angry she-bears to maul a band of impertinent boys who mocked his lack of hair (2 Kings 2:23-25). A cheeky burro balks, speaks in an understandable human tongue, and prevents a misguided seer from making an ass of himself (pun intended; Num. 22:22-40). A young man falls asleep while sitting in a window during one of Saint Paul's lengthy sermons (maxing out at midnight), falls three stories to his death while snoring, and is brought back to life amid the nighttime ruckus that surely ensued on the street below (Acts 20:7-12). A beloved disciple named Tabitha (Dorcas in the Greek; both names mean "gazelle")—known for lots of sacrificial running around for others, acts of service that matched her moniker—dies from a mysterious disease and then later breathes the air of new life right there on the second floor of the funeral home, surrounded by once weeping and now ecstatic widows (Acts 9:36-43). After praying for three weeks with no hint of an answer, a faithful captive in a foreign land finally receives a visit from an angelic messenger who assures the frustrated intercessor that his prayers have indeed been heard from the beginning, the tardy response blamed on a titanic divine wrestling match over the airspace of Persia with certain forces of darkness (Dan. 10:10-14).

Why are these fabulous stories (and many others like them) included in the Bible? And why do they captivate my daily attention? Did Thomas Jefferson have it right when he took scissors to these weird tales and pasted back together a version of the Bible that seemed better suited for reasonable people with common sense? What motivates me to place ultimate trust in the mysterious power revealed in these strange narratives, described in a hymn that Cindy and I sang one recent Tuesday at dawn?

> Mortal pride and earthly glory, sword and
> crown betray our trust;
> what with care and toil we fashion, tower
> and temple, fall to dust.

> But thy power, hour by hour, is my temple
> and my tower.[1]

Thinking back in various parishes I served, it's difficult to count how many young parents chose to decorate a new baby's nursery with Noah's gargantuan sailing vessel and smiling long-necked giraffes stretching into a cumulus cloud-filled sky bracketed by a multicolored rainbow.[2] I love the various theological nuances in that old story (Gen. 6–9). For example, the Hebrew word for "ark" in this watery narrative appears only here in the Old Testament and just one other place: to describe the little "basket" (Exod. 2:3) that saved baby Moses from the maniacal genocide of a nervous Egyptian Pharaoh who attempted to kill all Israelite baby boys because the enslaved foreigners were getting far too numerous and strong. The story of Noah and his miraculous ark—the massive floating basket filled with everything from baboons to bandicoots—evokes powerful themes of salvation and liberation. Christian writers would pick up on these same themes of a saving boat (the church) and the watery, liberating connection to baptism (see 1 Pet. 3:20–21). One could argue that any story of Jesus involving a floating mode of transportation is essentially a tale about life in the church and its saving mission. Since

1. Joachim Neander (1650–1680), "All My Hope on God Is Founded," in *Evangelical Lutheran Worship*, hymn 757 (verse two).
2. See Gen. 6:15. The ark is described here as a massive boat—150 yards long, twenty-five yards wide, and fifteen yards tall. If taken literally, roughly a floating football stadium and then some.

its inception in 1948, the World Council of Churches has used a boat as their main promotional logo.

I'm pretty sure, however, that parents of my pastoral acquaintance spent little time pondering the flipside darkness lurking below the colorful rainbow adorning the nursery wall above their new baby's crib: a global flood that killed all but a chosen few; a divine slaughter authored by the God who decided creation was all a big mistake. These old miraculous stories often raise questions about the nature of God and require ample time to unpack and explain, not only for adults but also older children who are paying attention. Why pause over them when there's enough darkness in the world already?

*

Well-intended folk have gone to great lengths to explain how the miracles in the Bible really happened. For example, the Red Sea was *actually* rather reedy, quite shallow, and not all that impressive to cross under the right circumstances should a decent desert wind begin to blow. Jesus, similarly, walked on a series of stepping stones on a rocky shelf of the Sea of Galilee in a nocturnal amble that only *seemed* buoyant to disciples who were needlessly afraid of joining Davy Jones and his locker in mistaken depths that weren't even over their heads.

The leader of a youth conference once passed around a single unglazed doughnut through a crowd of five hundred, instructing each participant to break off only a tiny taste. Forget hygiene here. The point of the exercise? If everyone was careful and no one was stingy, the whole crowd could receive a nibble. The *real* miracle in the eye-popping tale of a few loaves and fish that fed thousands is that people discovered the joy of sharing and probably pulled out stowed sandwiches from under their robes. Lo and behold, a version of the "Stone Soup" truth of communal largesse that Jesus, an inspiring preacher, really had up his sleeve.

These attempts at reasonable explanation are often referred to as a *reductionist* approach to reading the Bible—reducing a story to its bare elements of believability, assuming lavish embellishment in the original. Jeffrey John, an Anglican priest, describes two of his early teachers in England, one a literalist who took every miraculous detail in the Bible at face value, no questions asked, and the other a reductionist who removed all supernatural challenges in a story to its bare bones of communal acceptance by means of scientific explanation. "Both assumed that the most—indeed the only—interesting thing about the miracles was the question of what did or did not *happen*."[3] Neither approach seemed all that interesting for John, then a teenager.

It is undeniably true that the miracles in the Bible often pack a point beyond their literal paranormal proclivities. But erasing the unusual details of these ancient tales (and reducing their power to a collection of inoffensive morality truths) is ultimately satisfying for almost no one, even for skeptical friends like mine who chuckle at such attempts to placate their numerous biblical doubts. Airbrushing the oddities from the miracles,

3. Jeffrey John, *The Meaning in the Miracles* (Grand Rapids: Eerdmans, 2001), 4.

sanitizing their sensational twists and turns, is a rather presumptuous attempt to circumvent that which cannot be managed or edited by anyone even mildly open to various mysteries in our lives that defy easy explanation.

"You have not come to something that can be touched, a blazing fire . . . a voice whose words made the hearers beg that not another word be spoken to them" (Heb. 12:18–19). The author's mysterious claim here may be debatable, even rejected, but his belief in what the Nicene Creed would later call the "seen and unseen" is not clarified by attempting to arrive at a rational landing place that suits all inquiring minds. "For my thoughts are not your thoughts," says God in the book of Isaiah, "nor are your ways my ways" (55:8). I find that to be a comforting and hopeful statement even while recognizing that many of my friends do not.

There is more to signing on with this divine assertion, however, than simply dismissing very thoughtful people who demand proof according to the laws of science in order to assign credence to almost any event. Scientific inquiry, an inarguably valuable enterprise, has its own limits. "When most narrowly defined," writes Craig Keener, "science is about measurements and about what happens all the time under certain circumstances; it is not, however, about divine purpose or human meaning. Just as one does not weigh an object by its color or measure love by its height, the tools of science are designed only to explore particular sorts of questions."[4]

4. Craig S. Keener, *Miracles Today: The Supernatural Work of God in the Modern World* (Grand Rapids: Baker Academic, 2021), 13.

My friend Gary, a retired pastor, grew up with a father who struggled with alcoholism. Never physically violent, the father was a good man in most ways until he got drunk. And then the verbal barrage began, which was terrifying for a child. Late evening always surfaced great apprehension. Gary's mom gave him a book of Bible stories that never left his bedside. Around age ten, with Sunday School classmates, he received a New Testament with Psalms. "Every night I would read a psalm and a section from one of the gospels. After saying my prayers, I would kiss the Bible at the last page I read. Over the days, months, years, the oil from my face penetrated the onion-skin pages. This connection gave me a sense of comfort and security against any of my fears and a sense of God's presence. I still have that precious Bible and my mom's crocheted page marker."

This tender image of leaving the oily imprint of one's face upon the pages of the Bible, of receiving the power of ancient stories to confront the fears of the heart, is precisely how anyone encountering the Bible again after a long absence from its contents might approach the paranormal stories of Scripture that tend to confuse and confound.

"Mortal, eat this scroll that I give you and fill your stomach with it," God once said to a fearful prophet (Ezek. 3:3) who was then sent to shepherd difficult people, equipped only with a literary menu offering spiritual food "as sweet as honey." Perhaps Ezekiel actually chewed and swallowed the scroll, but he surely considered these words from outside himself, divinely gifted, with more than a passing glance. The prophet perceived these stories and tales of truth-telling to be as life-giving as his next meal for strength to face any coming challenge. The prophet Jeremiah, who regularly spoke truth to power, enjoyed a similar literary diet: "Your words were found, and I ate them, and your words became to me a joy and the delight of my heart" (15:16).

In a world filled with nameable (and also unnamed) fears, students of the Bible have sunk teeth into these old stories from every possible angle. Martin Luther was convinced of the ceaselessly revelatory nature of a story whose interpretation could never be exhausted, a "living word" that was turned over and over like a fine jewel and examined from various angles that brought abundant light and truth waiting to be excavated from a deep and bottomless mine. The same story might be interpreted in various ways by the same person over several decades depending upon life situation, age of the interpreter, or changing social context. Jewish rabbis call this midrash, the honoring of all details, even specific letters, pauses, and guesses at tenor and tone of a text. The eating of a story includes loving and attentive lingering over its ample ingredients. Rather than being repulsed by weird details, readers embrace such strange components as part of the overall recipe leading to wisdom and truth.

Young Gary's nocturnal encounter with the guiding power of these ancient and odd narratives offered him a practical rudder—a message that left a lasting imprint—toward safety in a situation utterly beyond his adolescent ability to manage or control. The stories he read at night shaped his moral compass and formed a courageous imagination capable of withstanding the unpredictable storms of his childhood. Gary's immersion in the Bible, daily consuming a menu of very old stories, nourished him (like Ezekiel and Jeremiah) for the challenging road ahead.

*

Come with me on a side detour to examine the life and ministry of one of the most interesting (and miraculously outlandish) characters in the entire Old Testament. You'll find him, the prophet Elisha, in 2 Kings, not to be confused with his mentor Elijah who ascends into heaven without dying in a fiery chariot (just after passing Elisha the prophetic mantle, a leadership garment) and is not heard from again until landing centuries later on a mountain with Moses to witness and comment upon the transfiguration of Jesus. Got all that? I can hear the soft and sometimes loud cackles of my skeptical friends who again question whether there are any limits at all to what I'll swallow and center my life around.

Perhaps your own skepticism resembles that of thoughtful parents in a powerful Stephen Dunn poem who are having second thoughts about dropping their daughter off each morning for Vacation Bible School at a nearby Methodist church. Any sort of faith they may have once possessed is now in the distant past, and they wonder whether even a short summer exposure to Jesus and the strange tales that shaped him might be harmful for their daughter's moral formation. "It had been so long since we believed, so long since we needed Jesus as our nemesis and friend," they confess in the poem. At home each evening, their daughter's newfound enthusiasm for the songs she learns and the Bible characters she discovers lead her parents to reluctantly conclude that it's impossible to teach disbelief to their child: "only wonderful stories, and we hadn't a story nearly as good."[5] If you're feeling similar misgivings about the biblically paranormal, please don't reject these odd stories at face value. Your doubts and skepticism can be powerful allies in getting at the deep truth of these old narratives and their staying power.

Take a look at the early chapters of 2 Kings. Elisha's impressive credentials include causing iron axe-heads to float (6:7), intercepting military messages telepathically (6:12), purifying rancid stew (4:40–41), and raising a boy from the dead who curiously sneezes seven times before rejoining his grateful mother (4:35). Elisha is the same bald savant, easily offended presumably, who calls forth the ire of two angry she-bears upon the heads of a pack of impertinent Cub Scouts (3:24). (That's how I like to imagine the lads, anyway.) I'm drawn to this strange and rather aloof man and his darkly amusing résumé, some of the vital components eluding easy interpretation. There's one miracle story within the corpus of his prophetic exploits, however, that's always struck me as a template for interpreting many other Bible tales of a strange and paranormal nature.

The story of Naaman (2 Kings 5:1–19) at first seems to be about a wealthy and leprous man in need of a health

---

5. Stephen Dunn, "At the Smithville Methodist Church," in *Local Time* (New York: Quill William Morrow, 1986), 53–55.

fix. He locates Elisha, the prophet does his thing, and a miraculous healing occurs in the Jordan River. But there are details in this story (like most miracle stories) that collectively reveal truth and healing in rather unexpected ways. Resembling bits of bread dropped along a trail in the forest, a good Bible story is full of hints leading to understanding that does not occur all at once, an intentional storytelling device undoubtedly employed by Jesus as he told parables whose meaning often took a while to detonate in a listener's imagination and life. I still don't have them fully figured out, and I've been pondering the tales for decades. This is often the nature of biblical narrative—layered, ponderous, and timeless.

Naaman was a commander (similar to a general) in the Aramaean army, "a great man" and "a mighty warrior." Imagine his lavishly decorated den, surely decked out with some sort of display featuring his military medals with several framed clippings from the *Aram Daily News* describing the general's battle prowess and field savvy. I suspect Naaman was used to getting his way with a snap of his fingers, his self-esteem rather elevated from regular applause and recognition. I'm reminded of an important man in one of my early parishes who would barge up to the church parsonage early in the morning in his baby blue Cadillac and blow the horn until one of the Honeycutt family occupants came out to gather his drive-by wisdom. Sometimes we hid behind the den curtains, peeping, giggling, and made a game of waiting him out. Naaman was like that—privileged, entitled, highly regarded.

Except the general had a medical problem he could not solve even with the best health care plan in all of

Aram. Leprosy tormented the proud man. He learns of Elisha, our bald buddy of bears, from an Israelite maid who suddenly recalls the prophet's prowess at healing such afflictions back home. With a royal letter of reference, Naaman travels to Israel with an impressive cache of gold, silver, and the best clothes that money could buy, all for a rather austere prophet who kept very little hanging in his closet.

Naaman rolls up in front of Elisha's house with his glittering entourage and honks his horn, so to speak, summoning the healer out to the curb. The prophet chooses to stay put and instead sends out to the great man a lowly messenger who says, "Go, wash in the Jordan seven times, and your flesh shall be restored and you shall be clean" (5:10). Clear, prescriptive, easy.

Is Naaman pleased with this simple health fix for his increasingly agonizing problem? No, he is not. The general hits the roof. "I thought that for me he would surely come out . . . wave his hand over the spot, and cure the skin disease!" (5:11). Naaman seems to say, Does this guy know who I am? His response reeks of entitlement in spades.

After disparaging the appearance of the Jordan River as a relative mudhole compared to the beautiful waterways back home, this proud and afflicted man finally dips his self-righteous ass in the river the prescribed number of times. Fun to imagine this scene for the cocky general, yes?

Naaman is healed and becomes a gushingly grateful and changed man. The leprosy has vanished. But at the end of the story, one has to pose an important question.

What was this man's primary affliction? A dermatological torment that was skin-deep? Or, something else, deeper down, even harder to heal?

This old story of healing has much in common with many of the miracle stories we'll examine in this book, revealing a timeless truth succinctly described in this ancient prayer: "Lord, let me know my end, and what is the measure of my days; let me know how fleeting my life is. . . . For I am your passing guest, an alien, like all my forebears" (Ps. 39:4, 12b). In other words, allow mortality and common finitude to shape how others perceive me and how to shape the living of these days.

The healed Naaman reminds me of a friend recovering from cancer treatments. We (two fathers) once had a conversation about his illness while watching our sons at a soccer game. "I'd never wish this on anyone," he began. "But my cancer has been a very weird gift, even knowing I may have only a few years left to live. It's woken me up to what a selfish bastard I've been so much of my life. It's helped me see my arrogance, my mistaken belief that I didn't need anyone. It's been an invitation to live each day as a miraculous gift. None of these insights would have occurred without the cancer. Never in a million years. I'm a changed man because of it."

Elisha, similarly, could see right through the general's stated need to a much deeper "leprosy" that afflicted his personality even more than this man's skin condition. A visible miracle occurs in his life, but also a deeper, unseen miracle.

This layered story brings to mind a miracle from early in the ministry of Jesus, the healing of an unnamed paralyzed man (Mark 2:1-12). Here the afflicted man does not suffer from an outsized arrogance like the general does, but the healing is similar in that it reaches deep down to probe an unstated need in any of us. Jesus is teaching one day "at home" and draws a crowd so large that the front-door entrance becomes blocked. Seeking a different access to the healer, four friends carry the man on a stretcher up a ladder to the roof, dig through the dirt and thatch, and lower their palsied friend to Jesus who says, rather shockingly, "Son, your sins are forgiven." The very first thing out of his mouth! If Jesus felt sorry for this man, we aren't told. In all the times I've been called to an emergency room setting, responding to a horrible accident where the victim has been injured through no fault of one's own, it's hard to imagine leaning down and whispering words of forgiveness before I chose to say anything else. The implication of such words would be clear and rather repulsive: the victim is surely responsible for the accident because of lax morality.

This story, like the story of Naaman, requires a decent amount of theological digging that mirrors the faithfulness of these four friends who dig through the roof to get to Jesus. A careful reader will take time to dig through the layers of meaning presented here. The obvious health need (leprosy earlier and now paralysis) is eventually addressed but almost as an afterthought. "Which is easier," Jesus asks of those shocked by his initial declaration, "to say to the paralytic, 'Your sins are forgiven,' or to say, 'Stand up and take your mat and walk'?" (Mark 2:9). I suppose one could also ask, Which is harder? Perhaps our personal answers will differ, but this is a wonderfully vexing question requiring a bit of time to faithfully think through.

In his ministry, Jesus clearly distances himself from the common (and false) linkage between personal mishap and moral failing. He once silenced questioners who seem to suggest some crass connection between a man's physical blindness and something the man (or his parents) may have done to cause it (John 9:1-3). Another time, Jesus's disciples wondered about two horrible events from the evening news (a gruesome murder and a collapsed tower) and their possible connection to sinful slipups committed by the unfortunate victims (Luke 13:1-5). Then and now, we search for easy explanations for suffering. Jesus will have none of this.

The paralyzed man miraculously walks, but not before Jesus seems to address something much deeper. There is a paralysis within my soul (within any of us) that's arguably even harder to heal. The spatial movement in this story (descent to Jesus and ascent to new life) is important. This is the language of baptism, often dramatized in the early church with steps leading down into the water and another set of steps leading up to a new community of friends willing to help carry us through any future affliction, regardless of the digging involved.

Above my writing desk as I compose these words is a long prayer list filled with names, people of various ages struggling with myriad challenges—infant breathing difficulties, breast cancer, drug addiction, ovarian cancer, bipolar disorder, Parkinson's disease. I bring their names before God the healer on a regular basis. Some have been on my list for many years and will probably remain there for many more. In a long pastoral career, there's a good chance that some sort of agonizing setback will afflict practically everyone in the congregation. The names intoned above my desk—and those offered in what seems like a steady stream of woe on Sunday mornings in worship spaces across the land—are important to remember and offer, regular prayers for healing and wholeness.

But the cumulative effect for anyone paying attention can be numbing and doubt-inducing. The young father, Brad, who cannot pray for his sick baby again comes to mind. Does God heal? Many? Some? What is the point of intercessory prayer? A sticky note of sorts to remind God of what the Creator surely already knows?

These questions lead me back to Naaman and his leprous affliction. And also to the paralyzed man whose pals dig through the roof and the strange words Jesus first poses to him. The actual miracles in these stories of ancient healing are important. But they (and many other miracle stories) lead me to conclude that the miraculous in the Bible may often grab our attention in a way that causes us to miss a wider truth, a deeper healing. Perhaps this is why Jesus is constantly telling his disciples to be quiet about the miracles he performed. He shushes people all the way to his crucifixion lest they perceive him to mainly serve as a magic man with a bag of tricks capable of making things instantly okay. We typically want results from invoking Jesus. Conversely, he seems to bore deeper to the heart, forming people capable of dealing with anything (including death itself) that might come their way. Are the miraculous stories true, factual in all respects? For those whose lives have been shaped (and healed) by the stories, the question may be missing the point. Did they really happen? A better question: Are the stories really happening in the lives of those who hear and heed them?

*

One of my favorite southern writers is Harry Crews (1935–2012) whose autobiography describing his early years is a regional classic. Born in southern Georgia near the Okefenokee Swamp, Crews is a funny, ribald, crass, and wise observer of the county that shaped him. He never knew his father who essentially worked himself to death while sharecropping land from first light to beyond sundown during the Great Depression. About the only thing that Crews inherited from his dad was a shoebox full of old photos that elicited stories told by other family members: the one about his father losing a testicle to gonorrhea after a short relationship with a Seminole girl who lived alone in the swamp; the one about a hot summer Florida Everglades employment gig when his dad was a teenager that included plenty of drinking, shooting alligators, and building the long highway known as the Tamiami Trail; and the one about another Bacon County resident and hog farmer, "Bad Eye" Carter, chopping the hand off a neighbor—the impudent hand resting, tauntingly, on a property-line fencepost before its severance—who dared to trespass on the land of a man whose axe stroke was accurate that day even if his vision was not. The wounded owner of the hand wanted to give his extremity a proper Christian burial, but Bad Eye wouldn't part with it. "This here hand belongs to me now, sumbitch. Found it on my land." Crews asks the reader,

> Did what I have set down here as memory actually happen? Did [these] men say what I have recorded, think what I have said they thought? I do not know, nor do I any longer care. My knowledge of my daddy came entirely from the stories I have been told about him, stories told me by my mother, by my brother, who was old enough when he died to remember him first hand, by my other kin people, and by the men and women who knew him when he was alive. . . . And I have lived with the stories of him for so long that they are as true as anything that ever actually happened to me.[6]

Harry Crews once removed the photos that shaped the stories of his father from the old shoebox and mounted them in a heavy leather album, to better preserve and observe them. After a week or so he took them out again, loose, unable to explain exactly why the photos did not belong there. "I believe now it was because a worn and vulnerable pasteboard box more accurately reflected my tenuous connection with him whom I never knew but whose presence has never left me, has always followed me just out of reach."[7]

6. Harry Crews, *A Childhood: The Biography of a Place* (New York: Penguin Books, 2022), 5.
7. Crews, *Childhood*, 7.

The stories passed down to Harry Crews concerning a father whom he never knew offer numerous commonalities to people like us who often wonder about the veracity of remarkable stories in the Bible, their purpose and whether they are to be trusted.

The word "miracle" is rarely used in the Bible. In John's Gospel, the favored word is "sign" (occurring seventeen times) and basically refers to an astonishing event that, like a catchy billboard, points to a wider and perhaps universal truth. A sign is a pointer that suggests something even more important than the action expressed or experienced. (We'll return to this idea in the next chapter while exploring several signs in Jesus's ministry described in the Gospel of John.) Elsewhere, the phrase "deed of power" is preferred, literally *dynamis* in the original Greek, from which the word "dynamite" is derived. Something explosive is about to occur, or (similar to a parable) will be planted for now in the hearts and minds of the listener or participant, gestating and set to detonate with slowly revealed meaning down the way.

Bruno Bettelheim (1903–1990), one of the most revered child psychologists of the twentieth century, is known for his work concerning the lasting power and attraction of fairy tales, especially in the imaginations of children. Miraculous Bible stories and fairy tales are not the same, even though many of my skeptical friends suggest just that. However, in his landmark book, *The Uses of Enchantment*, Bettelheim several times finds intersection between the two genres in that the stories (like those heard by Harry Crews) deeply shape one's moral formation and serve as spiritual touchstones in the journey toward maturity and discerning the distinction between right and wrong, light and darkness (and sometimes shades in between), developing a spiritual intuition to find a way through deep and foreboding woods inherent in anyone's life. The stories travel with us, consciously and unconsciously, mimicking the "living and active" nature of the Bible itself, "sharper than any two-edged sword . . . able to judge the thoughts and intentions of the heart" (Heb. 4:12). Like fairy tales, the miracle stories of the Bible often point to a greater truth and offer a way forward into an uncertain future. Each story, Bettelheim writes, "reflects some aspects of our inner world, and of the steps required by our evolution from immaturity to maturity. For those who immerse themselves in what the [story] has to communicate, it becomes a deep, quiet pool which at first seems to reflect only our own image; but behind it we soon discover the inner turmoils of our soul—its depth, and ways to gain peace within ourselves and with the world, which is the reward of our struggles."[8]

I'm thinking here of the strange story of Hagar's wilderness banishment in Genesis 21:8-20. Before the unusual and unexpected birth of Isaac to Abraham and Sarah, the aging couple deal with infertility issues. Sarah cannot conceive. Hagar—an Egyptian slave who belongs to Sarah—is given to Abraham by his initially understanding wife to serve as a surrogate. "Go in to my

8. Bruno Bettelheim, *The Uses of Enchantment: The Meaning and Importance of Fairy Tales* (New York: Vintage Books, 2010), 309.

31

slave-girl," Sarah says to her husband, "it may be that I shall obtain children by her" (16:2). Ishmael is born from this creative union. A world religion (Islam) traces its roots of origin back to Ishmael. The famous whaling novel, *Moby Dick*, invokes Ishmael in the first sentence of the book.

But there is tension between Hagar and Sarah throughout the pregnancy. Hagar "looked with contempt on her mistress" (16:4) and, several months pregnant, runs away into the wilderness to a spring of water near the ancient border of Egypt. Hagar is alone and afraid. She's returning home, escaping from the stares. But she's also tough and athletic, courageous, full of nerve and mettle for such a journey. Hagar, I'm convinced, could star in a Nike commercial.

An angel of the Lord locates Hagar beside the spring— unusual events are always occurring in the Bible near springs, pregnant with baptismal foreshadowing—and convinces Hagar to return to her scornful mistress. Her baby, the angel promises, will become "a wild ass of a man" (16:12). I'm unsure whether this prediction would comfort many pregnant moms of my acquaintance, but Hagar retraces her steps and returns, for now. On the return trip, she refers to God as "El-roi." I always think of the Jetsons and George's precocious cartoon son when I come upon this divine title, but here it means "God who sees." The spring, the sad trip into the wilderness, and the theme of sight (and insight) in this old narrative will be repeated for Hagar five chapters hence in Genesis.

Several years pass. Isaac (his name means "laughter" because his geriatric parents, almost ready for assisted living, found the pregnancy hilarious) is born unexpectedly, side-splittingly, and eventually becomes playmates with Ishmael (21:9). Sarah's old jealousy reemerges. She talks Abraham (who is "distressed" but not distressed enough, if you ask me) into banishing Hagar and the boy into the wilderness. Mom and child (Abraham's son!) are given bread and water, minimal provisions, and sent away to wander in the wilderness of Beersheba. Predictably, the water is consumed. Under an unrelenting desert sun, Hagar gives up and places her son under a bush to die, retreating "the distance of a bowshot" to avoid watching her son's death. She weeps aloud—a recurring wordless lament, a prayer, found throughout the Bible.

"God heard the voice of the boy" (21:17), a wordplay on Ishmael's name (literally, "God hears"). And then God asks a profoundly odd (and even amusing) question, given the circumstances: "What troubles you, Hagar?" Try to imagine Hagar's internal reaction here: What troubles me? What *troubles* me? How long do you have, All-Seeing One? This rather dark, divine cat-and-mouse exchange strikes me as a hallmark of Jewish humor, expressed even in very troubling times. If you plan on any sort of reentry into the world of the Bible, watch for it as a recurring literary device. I'm thinking of a blind beggar, Bartimaeus, who yells for Jesus at the top of his lungs in a crowd. Jesus's reply to this needy man has always struck me as rather preposterous: "What do you want me to do for you?" (Mark 10:51). Try to imagine this poor man's head-scratching internal response. Grateful, yes, but what else? I'm also thinking of two jaded guys heading away from town, pretty much punting the early church community, after the death of their leader. A stranger (Jesus incognito) starts to walk alongside. "Are you the only stranger in Jerusalem who does not know the things that have taken place there in these days?" (Luke 24:18) Please spend some time with Jesus's almost comical two-word reply: "What things?"

Hagar (like many who follow her in biblical experiences of divine visitation coupled with supernatural oddity) surely took time amid life-sapping thirst and hunger to raise her eyebrows at the seeming absurdity of a four-word query from heaven that either calls into question "all seeing" omniscience or reveals a key literary component of many similar miracle stories. I badly want to insert these words on the lips of our heroine: Well, what do you think is troubling me, O Divine Eye in the Sky?

Pay close attention to the first half of Genesis 21:19: "Then God opened [Hagar's] eyes and she saw a well of water." It's worth noting what is *not* stated here. There is no mention of God wiggling the divine nose and zapping a water source into existence there on the spot. Instead, Hagar's eyes were opened to see what was already there. Her grief and profound sense of impending loss prevented her from noticing what had been at her disposal all along had grief not clouded the solution to their predicament. The God who sees is about the business of helping others see. Is this a miracle? Very often, in this pastor's judgment, it's more of a miracle than bizarre events that seem obvious candidates for *The Twilight Zone*.

Hagar's story of sight and insight leads to a new life for Ishmael who "lived in the wilderness, and became an expert with the bow" (21:20). This mom's harrowing saga reminds me of a story Annie Dillard tells in one of her books about an Algonquin woman and her baby in the Arctic one deadly winter, left alone after everyone else had starved.

> The woman walked from the camp where everyone had died, and found at the lake a cache. The cache contained one small fishhook. It was simple to rig a line, but she had no bait, and no hope of bait. The baby cried. She took a knife and cut a strip from her own thigh. She fished with the worm of her own flesh and caught a jackfish; she fed the child and herself. Of course she saved the fish gut for bait. She lived alone at the lake, on fish, until spring, when she walked out again and found people.[9]

Divine miracles in the Bible often include human insight and specific internal change. The supernatural events of Scripture typically do not overwhelm our human experience and physical senses. The divine often coaxes, even teases. It's again worth noting C. S. Lewis's important insight: God "cannot ravish. He can only woo." Ravishing the intellect, completely overwhelming and removing my skepticism (yes, even pastors are blessed with doubts), would leave me fundamentally less than human. God is indeed after your hidden heart but refuses to create mindless Stepford disciples in the process.

9. Annie Dillard, *The Writing Life* (New York: Quality Paperback Books, 1989), 12–13.

Are the miracle stories in the Bible true? Did they really happen? I'm with Harry Crews here (and many others). The stories are true to the extent that they lead a reader or listener to deep truth. In an era of outright lying in politics masquerading as truth, with conspiracy theories holding an outsized role in the imaginations of the American electorate, the abiding promise found in these old miracle narratives offers no small alternative to all the false claims of fake news.

Just before his arrest and crucifixion in John's Gospel, Jesus offers a powerful promise to his disciples: "Those who love me will keep my word, and my Father will love them, and we will come to them and make our home with them" (14:23). In all their curiosity (and even compelling confusion), these old stories—ingested into our lives (like the prophets) and slowly masticated into the memory—provide a portable resting place, a home, for the divine to shape and change any of us.

"Let there be light," let there be wilderness, wildebeest, and black widow spiders. God oddly *speaks* a new world into being (in all of its astonishing variety) in the Bible's opening chapter (Gen. 1). God also speaks into being, through the details and grist of the miracle stories, people newly equipped to live in such a complex world.

2

Jesus the Miracle Worker

The Messiah was not going to save the world by miraculous, Band-Aid interventions. . . . Rather, it was going to be saved by means of a deeper, darker, left-handed mystery, at the center of which lay his own death.

—Robert Farrar Capon

Rather than be the great palliative for people, Jesus put most of his followers in greater pain than they would have had if he had not called them.

—William H. Willimon

'll admit it. Read any of the Four Gospels associated with the ministry of Jesus and the effect, especially for someone new to the Bible (or perhaps returning to it), may often seem like encountering sensational headlines from tabloids such as *The National Enquirer*:

> "Local Magician Transforms Wedding Wine Bar"
> "Medium Peers into Shady Lady's Past at Town Watering Hole"
> "Mysterious Sea-Boy Feeds Thousands with Big Mac and Fries"
> "Man Blind from Birth Praises Vanishing Faith Healer"
> "Mummified Corpse Speaks and Eats"

I've chosen the Gospel of John (and the five stories associated with these headlines) for the general framework for this chapter introducing the paranormal ministry of Jesus. Subsequent chapters will address more specific miracle genres, including those occurring in nature and others associated with healing from rather bizarre demonic possession. All along the way, I'll keep in mind your skepticism and questions I've heard posed by friends and parishioners, perhaps echoing a few of your own.

You will soon discover that John's testimony about Jesus may seem like an odd place to start. This gospel is dense, multilayered, and filled with long conversations laden with symbolism and double (even triple) entendres. The straightforward prose of the first three gospels—commonly known as "the Synoptics" because the trio of testimonies generally see eye to eye on Jesus's length of ministry and teaching content—may seem like a better place to begin our exploration, especially since most scholars believe they came first. I'm convinced, nonetheless, that John trains our senses to look for various details, similar to an amateur sleuth, that with time and practice form important interpretive abilities that translate well to the tackling of any miracle story found anywhere in the Bible.

Again, miracles (especially in John) are often referred to as "signs," pointers. Pointing to what? And here is the mysterious and marvelous nature of John's Gospel. These signs will *not* render the ministry of Jesus immediately obvious and tied up with a clear and unmistakable bow. Jesus wants us to dig. (Recall the story of the paralytic from the previous chapter whose friends dug through the roof to get to Jesus.) Like your best teachers from the past, Jesus will not serve up easy answers or an immediate path to understanding. Insight often comes in a slow (and even slippery) way with Jesus, because he wants our acquired wisdom to last, interpreting the past and leading us into the future. This is not a fast-food endeavor.

An open Bible (preferably one with annotations) will help as we begin our search. I'll be using the New Revised

Standard Version (NRSV), but any Bible will do. Lift one from your motel room if need be. The Gideons would be delighted if you took it. I'll include a miracle maxim to begin each section and offer comments upon each of the five stories I've chosen. By the end of the chapter, you'll have five general maxims to apply to any future miracle story that you'll encounter in the ministry of Jesus.

1. John 2:1–11: A Sign That Points to a Life Filled with Joy and Ferment

Several years ago, I heard Morris Dees (former director of the Southern Poverty Law Center) speak at Emory and Henry College in Virginia. Dees told a story about his fifth-grade teacher, Mrs. Jones, who loved the Bible and used it often in class. She was adamantly opposed to any use of alcohol for any purpose, recreational or religious, and regularly spoke of this stance to her young charges. Morris, by his own admission, was a rather sassy ten-year-old. One day, after another in-class homily from Mrs. Jones about the deplorable evils of alcohol, Morris raised his hand.

"My pastor just had a sermon the other Sunday about Jesus turning all that water into wine at the wedding in Cana of Galilee. My daddy says that must have been some party. What do you make of that old story?"

Mrs. Jones let the question sit a moment and looked out at twenty-five sets of eager and impressionable eyes. "Well, now. We all wish that Jesus hadn't of done that, now don't we?" she replied.

Very early in John's Gospel—in some ways setting the tone for all that follows—Jesus and his disciples are at a wedding "on the third day," a possible suggestion that this episode in the life of Jesus points even further to another story of a man who rose from the grave on the third day, life from death, the ultimate resurrection party. I've always been rather amused by the attendance of Jesus and his friends at this matrimonial celebration. Did they bring gifts? Attend the groom's party the night before? Dance the Palestinian equivalent of the Electric Slide?

Jesus is often portrayed in the Gospels as a rather dour and serious man. There are instances of people laughing *at* him (Matt. 9:24) but not a single story of Jesus throwing back his head with a teeth-baring, side-splitting guffaw. Such laughter surely occurred in his ministry. The guy was human, after all, and the instances of him slyly toying a bit with his followers are many. For example, the man is mistaken for a gardener (John 20:15) in one of his resurrection appearances. Rembrandt portrays this scene with Jesus in full garden getup, maybe his playful costume suggesting a symbolic connection to ancient garden of Eden references in the Bible's opening chapters, new life and new chances.

Anyway, I like imagining him at this wedding, just hanging out and having fun with his friends. Mary, his mom, was in attendance. One extrabiblical source suggests that she was an aunt to the bridegroom. If this is true, then Mary must have had something to do with the reception, perhaps in charge of the beverages. This might explain her rather nervous declaration to her son in verse 3 of this old story: "They have no wine."

The Beverage Barn was closed on the weekends, and the bar is bare. Mary was facing something of a social faux pas. She is, of course, anxious and maybe a bit panicked about the lack of refreshments, but one facet of John's Gospel (watch for it, repeatedly) is that rather innocuous statements carry more freight and meaning than the obvious. This gospel is virtually swimming in potent metaphors. Linguists call this "polyvalence," a word you can use when you go on *Jeopardy!* "Light" hardly ever means just one thing in this gospel. Same for "bread." Same for "water."

They have no wine. This short four-word declaration certainly describes this first-century wedding challenge, but also something much deeper below the surface for any future reader of the story. A lack of wine is a re-markably apt description of so many relationships, marriages, and lives: no sparkle, no pizzazz, no passion. Wine "makes the timid brave and the reserved amorous," writes Frederick Buechner. "It loosens the tongue and breaks the ice, especially when served in a loving cup. It kills germs. As symbols go, it is a rather splendid one."[1]

Jackson Browne's folk song, "Running on Empty," comes to mind when thinking of Mary's literal and symbolic wedding quandary. Perhaps there's a bit of temporary exhilaration to such a state. One of my favorite *Seinfeld* episodes is where Kramer test-drives a car with a fuel

---

1. Frederick Buechner, *Wishful Thinking: A Seeker's ABC* (San Francisco: HarperCollins, 1993), 120.

needle that flirts dangerously with the big E on the gas gauge. Knowing he needs to exit or run out of gas, Kramer floors it past the exit anyway. Both he and the car salesman explode in laughter, loving the danger of it all.

Mary leans over to her son and says, with some urgency, "They have no vino." There is perhaps no more loaded statement in this entire gospel of loaded statements. Mary is certainly talking about a beverage, but this story—the first of Jesus's signs (pointing to something greater)—is about far more than a beverage. Again, please watch for this in the miracle stories of Jesus: a deeper meaning below the surface of the obvious.

Six stone jars are sitting nearby, each holding twenty or thirty gallons. You can do the math—a vast amount of wine, reams of *Reunite*. Merlot, chardonnay, Shiraz, take your pick. Yet there's even more wine here than first meets the eye.

In one of his books that translates the Gospels with a southern flair, Clarence Jordan (1912-1969)—a farmer and Greek scholar who founded an interracial Christian community in south Georgia when it was very dangerous to do so—points out an interesting twist on a Greek word in verse 8 of this wedding story, "to draw out." This word literally means "to draw water from a well with a bucket" and will be used two chapters hence in John 4 (we'll soon get to this story) to describe the woman at the well whose bucket helps quench the thirst of Jesus on a very hot day.

Jordan maintains that this one word offers a marvelous twist on a familiar story. Here's his translation, directly from the Greek, with a southern flair: "He told the servants, 'Fill the crocks with water,' and they filled them up to the brim. Then Jesus said, '*Now* let your bucket down and draw up some for the emcee.' They fetched it. When the emcee tasted the water-become-wine, he didn't know where it came from, though the servants who had bucketed it up knew."[2]

In other words, the *entire well* had turned to wine, according to Jordan, not the water in the jars. The gist of this compelling interpretation is that you don't just have 180 gallons of wine when Jesus is around. You've got *endless wine*, a bottomless wellful of wine that does not run dry.

This image undoubtedly was not lost on another Baptist pastor who knew Jordan. Martin Luther King Jr. did not help change the world because he was convinced that people, deep down, were basically good and capable of racial equality alone. He did not help change the world with seven core convictions dear to his heart, a claim I once heard at a MLK rally attended mostly by liberal white people who held hands and swayed to some nice peace songs. King, conversely, brought about radical change through his radical commitment to Jesus (often surprisingly ignored when we invoke King's accomplishments), drawing upon Christ's deep well of endless wine that can indeed transform a broken world.

This first miracle maxim in John's Gospel is foundational for the other four that will follow: life with Jesus

---

2. Clarence Jordan, *The Cotton Patch Version of Matthew and John* (El Monte, CA: New Win, 1970), 105.

is described in this story by a bottomless well of wine leading to both joy and deep ferment. But so what? ask my skeptical friends. And maybe you're asking the same question, or a similar one posed by a young college student to his teacher, theologian Douglas John Hall: "*So what I want to know is, Why Jesus? In the first place, I'm not convinced even believing in God is possible today. Why make it even more complicated by asking people to believe in Jesus?*"[3]

One response to this simple and excellent question is found by looking at what follows this story in John's Gospel (2:13–25), filling out chapter 2. Jesus enters the temple and discovers that his "Father's house" is filled with charlatans; money changers turning the faith into a religious sideshow. Jesus makes a whip of cords and drives out the whole sordid economic circus. (Rembrandt, by the way, was so taken with this scene that he painted a halo above Jesus's *hands* holding the holy whip, rather than the traditional halo around his head.) This defiant act did not go over well with the temple leaders. Those in charge began to build a case against Jesus.

There is a connection between these two stories—wine at a wedding and all hell breaking loose in the temple. With Dr. King, one discovers fairly quickly that fighting injustice in the world and working for real change requires something more than one's own best efforts. The wine of Jesus will lead to real ferment with tables turned over and people getting ticked. Read

3. Douglas John Hall, *Why Christian? For Those on the Edge of Faith* (Minneapolis: Fortress, 1998), 17.

again the quotation by Will Willimon that opens this chapter: "Rather than be the great palliative for people, Jesus put most of his followers in greater pain than they would have had if he had not called them."[4] Following Jesus, authentic discipleship, will ensure (as someone, slyly, once put it) that a disciple is willing to risk "looking good on wood." Real ferment, substantive change requiring a passionate commitment to the ways of Jesus, cannot be realized for the long haul without the regular refreshment of a deep well of wine from a source outside ourselves.

Why Jesus? Partly because we need someone to keep pushing us toward the injustices of this world and refreshing us when we're exhausted, out of gas, running on empty. The Christian sacramental tradition offers this very back and forth in the various components of the Sunday liturgy, even though it's sometimes missed by parishioners more interested in maintaining the building.

A congregation I served in downtown Columbia, SC, was once joined to another church now located less than one-half mile away, just around the corner. The two churches divided in 1886. The issue? The use of sacramental wine (rather than grape juice) in celebrating Holy Communion on Sundays during an era when the Temperance Movement raged around the country. The argument became so heated that a new congregation was formed. This is the sort of division that causes my

4. William H. Willimon, *Why Jesus?* (Nashville: Abingdon, 2010), 64.

skeptical friends to roll their eyes and have nothing to do with church affiliation. In some ways, I can't blame them. It's just the sort of narrow focus on making Sunday mornings look just right while ignoring glaring injustices just outside the church door that often drove me crazy as a pastor.

But what if this old story of Jesus turning water into wine is about more than a beverage? My friend Rodney Clapp, a writer and editor, tells a story about his hometown Episcopal congregation and their building project, which included new carpet in the church nave. The carpet would build up a fairly strong static electricity charge caused by the friction from the shoes of parishioners. When someone knelt and sipped from the metal wine chalice, the communicant would often receive quite a jolt.

I love this image. Jesus turns water to wine at a wedding to bring both joy *and* ferment—joy in the life of community, like a fun nuptial gathering, but always sending partygoers back out into the surrounding community with a jolt of justice and grace to help those left out of the festivities. Jesus brings pizzazz and panache to a life like mine, prone to the sedentary.

Early in John's Gospel, a team of nervous fact finders heads out to an old river and peppers John the Baptist with a series of questions (John 1:19–28). "Who are you?" the inquisitors ask, right off the bat. Ballpoint pens and tape recorders are at the ready, eager to catch the baptizer in some theological slipup.

"I am not the Messiah," John responds. For those of us who sometimes seek to serve in such a role with various friends and family members, few words are as sweet.

Why Jesus? Let this first miracle maxim percolate a bit. *He fills his people with the joy of new wine from a bottomless well where all are invited to drink deeply.*

2. John 4:1–42: A Sign That Points to a Fully Exposed, Accepted, and Forgiven Past

Jesus sits down with a woman at an old well. They chat at some length. This verbal exchange near an ancient source of hydration (again, keep baptism and new life in mind anytime you encounter water in the New Testament) is the longest recorded conversation between Jesus and another person in any of the Gospels—longer than anything he said to his disciples, longer than any talk he had with his mom. Catechumens (candidates for baptism) in the early church pored over this and other lengthy stories in John for months as they reflected upon life in the church and whether they were ready to give their lives in service to such a man. Recall the divine admonition for Ezekiel and Jeremiah to "eat this book," ingesting the details and nuances of Scripture as a menu of nourishment and sustenance for the journey ahead. There are lots of ingredients in this old story to munch upon.

Jesus goes out of his way to reach this woman. Consult a map in the back of the Bible you're using. Locate place names mentioned in the verses prior to chapter 4 in John. We're told that Jesus "had to go through

Samaria" (4:4) on his way home to Galilee. Well, not really. His chosen route was not the quickest way back. Jesus doesn't arrive at this well thanks to time-saving MapQuest directions. This encounter is definitely out of his way, intentionally, not (as it seems to be in many cases) by chance.

It is "about noon" (4:6), quite hot.[5] Jesus is pretty bushed from the walk. The disciples have gone into town to buy food, leaving him alone at the well. He strikes up a conversation with a local woman. Upon the disciples' return (4:27), they'll be rather shocked that their leader is chatting with a woman in public. And a *Samaritan* woman, on top of that. Jews like Jesus maintained a long-running feud with Samaritans that stretched back to an ancient argument over where to best worship God. If you know the story of the good Samaritan (Luke 10:25-37), you'll recall that Jesus casts an unpopular outsider as the hero. Tack the descriptor "good" onto any person you tend to find morally repulsive, have them save the day, and the story packs quite a punch. So far, back at the well, if I'm counting correctly, Jesus has admirably crossed three sets of tracks involving geography, gender, and ethnicity.

The woman has a bucket. She starts to draw water. Please recall the previous story and the same verb (2:8) that suggests a veritable well of wine. The stories are further connected when Jesus says, mysteriously,

5. Jesus will be crucified at this hour at the end of John's Gospel, in part for the mounting theological and cultural improprieties akin to those revealed in this story.

"Everyone who drinks of this water will be thirsty again, but those who drink of the water that I will give them will never be thirsty" (4:13-14). Endless wine, endless water.

Here is evidence of a long-standing sacramental tradition stretching back to the years of the early church. The woman expresses a desire to have a bit of that water (and, by extension, that wine) in her life. If the story ended right there—close curtain, cue applause—it would be something of an inclusion miracle given local norms and context. To be honest, I really *want* the story to end right there at 4:15. Surprisingly (and thankfully), it doesn't.

In many churches across America, across denominational lines, hangs a picture of Jesus painted by an artist from Chicago, Warner Sallman (1892-1968). Five hundred million copies of the painting have been sold. I grew up with this painting on the wall of my childhood Sunday school classroom. No other painting, I suspect, has shaped the American imagination concerning Jesus more than this one. He seems kind, gentle, absolutely nonthreatening and looking like he's just back from a Clairol makeover, polished and sanitized, easy on the eyes, all accepting, never offensive to anything or anyone.

The problem with this painting and this common image of Jesus is that he was consistently offending people. As a working pastor, I used to tell parishioners that if they're never offended by Jesus, then I'd have to conclude that they've stopped reading the man with any frequency or consistency. Of course Jesus was offensive. He was consistently pissing people off by what he said and did. He often seems rude (manners be damned) on behalf of God's intrusion into the lives of people who've hidden things their entire lives behind many masks. (And that, of course, includes this writer.) If you're ticked off by Jesus when reading the Bible, never fear. You're on the right track.

The woman at this old well has made great strides in understanding her need for the living water that Jesus seems to be offering. She wants what he has. "Give me [your] water, so that I may never be thirsty." I commend her. Many church people of my acquaintance haven't gotten this far. But here comes the intrusive, seemingly rude, paranormal unpleasantness from one dubbed a gentle, nonthreatening shepherd, one as consistently kind as your grandmother bearing a tray of milk and cookies.

Still at the well, the man with X-ray eyes asks to meet this woman's husband, knowing she's had more spouses than Elizabeth Taylor, not including the guy she's shacked up with at the moment. Talk about your cringe-worthy moment. Why bring this up now? Why does Jesus find this woman's past any of his business? Isn't Jesus aware of how to add followers to his movement, making discipleship as pain and cost-free as possible?

In the Lutheran liturgy, at the very first of the service on most Sunday mornings, the congregation offers a corporate confession soon after assembling. Part of the confession addresses a God "to whom all hearts are open, all desires known, and from whom no secrets are hid."[6] *No secrets!* Gracious, couldn't I keep a few?

In the rubrics of the confession is a fine-print instruction in red letters: "Silence is kept for reflection." It took me awhile as a pastor to learn that a lot was going on in that short silence—profound and poignant reflections upon past mistakes, missed opportunities, wounding words, and hope for the future. On behalf of God (that right there enough to make a pastor's knees knock), I'd soon proclaim corporate forgiveness and absolution to the congregation. But I learned to let the silence linger first. People get out of bed and come to worship on Sunday mornings for a variety of reasons, but perhaps primarily we all arrive at church to receive forgiveness and deal with the past. Masks stripped away, we stand before God with all our baggage, all our mistakes, all our hopes for restoration and change.

Part of the miracle of this story is that this woman encounters someone who can see right through her, sees all of her mistakes. You'd think this might be an embarrassing and shameful moment for her. But the exact opposite is true. She's ecstatic that she's met someone who knows her so completely and accepts her anyway. Her joy even extends to neighbors who've probably sat in judgment of her failings for many years. "Come see a man who told me everything I've ever done! He cannot be the Messiah, can he?" (4:29).

6. *Evangelical Lutheran Worship* (Minneapolis: Augsburg Fortress, 2006), 94.

Far from feeling bound by her past, this woman feels absolutely liberated, utterly unburdened from meeting a man who seems to know everything about what she's kept hidden and masked, perhaps now doing handstands before her nosy neighbors in the public square. "The Messiah," writes Barbara Brown Taylor, "is the one in whose presence you know who you really are—the good and bad of it, the all of it, the hope in it."[7] That, if you think about it, is a rare gift.

One popular notion of Jesus is that he serves as a quasi-Gotcha God, lurking in the shadows of our lives, waiting for us to goof up, and then lowers the boom on our waywardness. I've always loved a story that occurs toward the very end of this same gospel (John 21:1-14). After the death of Jesus, the disciples have a hard time holding the early Christian community together. Seven disciples, by my count, are sitting around one evening. Several are missing. I imagine them having a few beers, reminiscing. Peter, with nothing better to do, says, "I am going fishing." This man and his friends have been given clear marching orders by their deceased leader. They now have a new vocation—fishing for people, not flounder. Peter knows this; he goes back to his old job anyway.

Curiously, Peter is fishing in the buff that night (21:7), not a stitch of clothing. Maybe he's hot. Peter and company catch nothing, not a guppy. Standing on the beach the next morning is a man who knows Pe-

7. Barbara Brown Taylor, "Face to Face with God," *Christian Century*, February 28, 1996, 227.

ter completely, who catches this exposed disciple with his pants down, so to speak, out doing something he's clearly not supposed to be doing. Recognizing Jesus, surely flustered and embarrassed, Peter pulls on his pants and jumps into the water. He's excited to be reunited with this man who seemingly has X-ray eyes. But I also suspect that Peter's rather nervous, caught, probably waiting to be admonished. What Peter finds instead is a fire, a mess of fish, and about the best invitation a guilty conscience might hear: "Come and have breakfast" (21:12). Jesus "took the bread and gave it to them." Shades of Holy Communion, divine acceptance, radical forgiveness.

I'm told that a bar in Reno, Nevada, has bathrooms at the top of a long and noticeable flight of stairs. The women's room includes a painting of a naked man whose genitals are covered by a hinged metal fig leaf kept in place with a coiled spring. Unbeknownst to the occupant of this restroom, a bell rings in the bar below whenever the fig leaf is raised for private inspection. As the unsuspecting woman descends the stairs, bar occupants applaud in a rousing cheer, exposing her solitary peeking. Humorous? But also caught, humiliated, embarrassed. It probably says a lot about this bar that the men's room does not include a similar trap.

Jesus does not probe the past of this woman at a well in order to embarrass or shame her. She's undoubtedly experienced enough of both. He looks into her life, "the all of it, the hope in it," allowing the penetrating light and acceptance of his love to fully include whatever failures and indiscretions have shaped or wounded her.

Could it be true that anyone desires more than anything else to be known so completely and fully with shortcomings exposed, all disguises dropped, still accepted and loved and included? "He told me everything I have ever done" (4:39). It's impossible to know the tenor of her voice here, but I hear liberation, relief, and joy.

My friend whom I'll call Jonah committed a horrible crime several decades ago. Jonah grew up in a very poor household in the lower part of rural South Carolina with a mom who tried to hold her family together but often couldn't. Leaving for hours at a time when Jonah was small, she would sometimes bury him in a hole up to his neck so that her son would not run away. How this must have shaped my friend I can only imagine. Jonah was diagnosed with schizophrenia as a teenager. Medication helped. When he stopped taking his medicine, Jonah heard voices telling him to do awful things. He raped and murdered a woman one night and now serves a sentence of life in prison without hope of parole.

When I first met Jonah over fifteen years ago (through my daughter, then a public defender), he was on death row and regularly received visits from local ministers who reminded him that he was bound for hell anyway, so why not give up and be executed, getting it over with. On our first meeting, I'd never met a human being who seemed more hopeless and forlorn. He was aware of his crime, had been told some of the details, but had no memory at all of what had occurred. Jonah wanted to die. He was more than ready to walk to the state's electric chair. "I deserve death," he told me. "An eye for an eye. Doesn't it say that in the Bible?"

Slowly, through visits and many letters, Jonah began to recall Bible stories of acceptance and new beginnings that he'd learned in church as a child with his grandmother. His defense attorney, mitigation investigator, and social workers all saw value and potential in Jonah. They helped to reconnect him with an estranged brother, made sure his medication was properly administered, and advocated for him to get off death row. Today Jonah leads a Bible study in his prison unit and helps men who are new to prison life in a program called Roommate 101. He freely admits that he's the person he is today because people took time to love and accept him, those who even knew exactly what he'd done in his past.

"The water that I will give," Jesus tells an isolated woman at a well, "will become in them a spring of water gushing up into eternal life" (4:14). I've always been fascinated with springs, fresh water from an unseen source. On my long backpacking trip on the Appalachian Trail from Maine to Georgia (more on that journey in the next chapter), marked springs described in my guidebook trail data allowed a hiker to walk to the next source of refreshment with confidence. I encountered only one dry spring in the twenty-one hundred miles of the trail's length. In the early 1980s, the intestinal parasite giardia was far less of a concern. I'd never treat water if I was confident that nothing was above the spring, possibly fouling the source. It was fascinating and humbling to learn sometimes that a certain spring was the very source of a river formed by multiple cascades and creeks flowing at an elevation far below the high ridgeline I was standing upon.

Being fully known and loved by Jesus, and being fully known and loved by other human beings, releases in any of us a spring of water flowing from a hidden source where our worth, value, and purpose reside. Discovering this truth and learning to live it is something of a miracle.

An interesting detail from this old story of a woman at an ancient well: she "left her water jar and went back to the city" (4:28). She was now part of a new story that included portable water giving her confidence to face anything, even her past—the truth and power of baptism. She went back to a city that had surely rejected her with news of a man who knew her past in all of its once-embarrassing detail. Jesus delves into this woman's past not to judge her but instead to liberate her. This is the language of baptism.

It could be interesting to ponder the questions Jesus might pose to any of us at this old well—the mistakes we hide from, the incidents that still bring both embarrassment and regret. I'm pretty sure I know the questions Jesus would pose to me. We all (believer and skeptic alike) need someone who knows us so completely, helping us to make sense of and move beyond the paralyzing elements of our past.

"I am he, the one who is speaking to you," says Jesus to this woman (4:26). In the Greek, the first three words of this statement point to a single name, I AM, the divine name once revealed to Moses at a burning bush (Exod. 3:14). This voice, the church claims, still speaks to anyone with welcome and transformation of any past mistake. That, if you ask me, is a miracle worth pondering at some length.

3. John 6:1–15: A Sign That Points to Abundance in Community Where All Are Fed

You've noticed by now that the signs Jesus is performing attract ever larger crowds—some are curiosity seekers, some (local religious leaders) feel threatened by the attention he's receiving, and some need tangible help. Prior to one of his most famous miracles, Jesus hops in a boat and sails to "the other side" (6:1) of the sea. The man, I suspect, needs a break. One version of this same story (Matt. 14:13–21) is introduced by a report of the beheading of John the Baptist, a relative of Jesus; let's call him a cousin. The disciples collect cousin John's headless body, bury it, and then share the grisly news with Jesus. Upon hearing such a bizarre and violent report, Jesus retreats by water to "a deserted place by himself" (Matt. 14:13).

I can see him rowing, full of sadness, recalling childhood memories, trying to get away and grieve, but then encountering a crowd of needy thousands waiting on the far beach at his retreat site. We're told he had "compassion" (Matt. 14:14) for all these waiting people, a rare Greek word that literally means that your guts have been turned inside out with emotion. In Matthew, Jesus feeds the same thousands even with the shadow of a headless cousin clouding the man's psyche. For my money, it's hard to determine the more impressive miracle. Feeding so many people, or pushing down so much emotion before doing so. John's version of this sign does not mention the beheading context, but it's worth keeping this Stephen King–like detail in mind. Jesus, the church claims, was both divine and human. He needed to get away—often retreating, often interrupted.

Returning to John's version of this feeding miracle, you'll soon encounter a trio of curious verses that call out for a bit of commentary.

> When he looked up and saw a large crowd coming toward him, Jesus said to Philip, "Where are we to buy bread for these people to eat?" He said this to test him, for he himself knew what he was going to do. Philip answered him, "Six months wages would not buy enough bread for each of them to get a little." (John 6:5–7)

The disciples seem a bit nervous in this scene. Think about your last dinner party and how much effort you put in to entertain a single table of *invited* guests. Now imagine five thousand uninvited souls knocking on your door for some supper. It's like my entire town of Walhalla, SC (population 4,685), and then some hearing about a picnic in my backyard. You can only stretch hotdogs so far.

But Jesus sits there as calm as a cucumber and says to Philip, surely with a pause for dramatic effect, "I wonder how we're gonna feed all these people?" That line alone, if I'd been there, may have left me wondering about Jesus and his sanity. But the reader is privy to more: the mind of Jesus, editorial information that Philip did not have. "He said this to test him, for he himself knew what he was going to do."

Don't skip over this line too quickly, no anomaly with Jesus. This seems to be a character trait—the man's a jester, a tease, a tester, in several places in the Gospels. What intrigues me is the obvious follow-up question—*Why?* Why does Jesus behave this way so consistently?

Here's a bit of truth for all new (and returning) skeptical students of the Bible: Jesus refuses to serve up a soufflé of universal principles that will magically fix all of life's problems. He is not going to make it all obvious for us. He's going to tease and nudge and drop small pieces of bread along the path, refusing to provide instant solutions. This is hard for us to get used to in a world of instant everything. "My life was a mess. I was on my fourth marriage. I'd maxed out seventeen credit cards and was addicted to Snickers bars and Cheez-Its. And then I found Jesus and everything was okay, overnight." Maybe, but I suspect such instant bliss is rare.

A little boy comes forward with just a meager amount of food: five small barley loaves and a couple of perch. "Make the people sit down" (6:10), says Jesus, and they all did so in "a great deal of grass." These images might surface old memories (from a funeral, from your childhood) of the Twenty-Third Psalm—"He makes me lie down in green pastures." Sitting down at the feet of

Jesus for any length of time, listening to his perspective, can cause strange and unexpected things to happen in anyone's life, but not all at once.

The story says that "Jesus took the loaves, and when he had given thanks, he distributed them" (6:11) to all in the crowd. These words closely resemble the ancient Words of Institution, the words a priest or pastor offers in conjunction with the Sunday celebration of the Lord's Supper. The Greek word for "give thanks" at this mountainside picnic is *eucharistein*—a word that gave birth to one of the names for this holy meal: Eucharist.

All eat, "as much as they wanted" (6:11), with plenty of leftovers—there on the grass, satisfied, sated. Think Archie Bunker reclining in his Barcalounger with a toothpick. This meal was not a shared snack. It was a feast. And yes, plenty of attempts exist to explain away the paranormal profundity of it all. Recall the shared doughnut at the youth conference in the previous chapter. Recall the Stone Soup hypothesis. This, however, is a generous meal of provided abundance, not a repast featuring restrained reactions to scarcity or a supper of creative, inspired sharing.

There was a great couple—Vernon and Ruby, local farmers and generational orchardists—in my first parish out of seminary in the Shenandoah Valley. I once helped Vernon slaughter a pig, an interesting and odorous process lasting a couple of days. One of the favorite Honeycutt family photos features our oldest daughter, Hannah, wide-eyed and hardly a year old, with assistance, sitting on the back of Ruby's favorite cow.

One day, we came home to the parsonage and found a bushel of carrots in the carport. A *bushel* of carrots will feed a family for a while, especially a family of three. How could we possibly use so many carrots? An insane number of root vegetables exceeding any foreseeable salad needs for months into the future. Nobody had left a note, but I knew it was Vernon. Was he crazy or something? No, just generous and tremendously grateful for the wonder of land, seed, and soil. We thanked him and ate what we could.

"You open your hand," claims an old prayer about God's largesse, "satisfying the desire of every living thing" (Ps. 145:16). The story of Jesus feeding thousands illustrates this ancient claim in microcosm. I hear your objections: rampant and recurring global famine; thousands of unfed refugees looking for shelter and their next meal; the hypocrisy of a pastor with a church pension plan daring to defend God's grandiose generosity that seems to have gone missing in so many cases. This old story raises a very good question (one I'll return to in a future chapter): If Jesus fed thousands back then with a little boy's little lunch and a magical wave of his hand, why doesn't he instantly feed similar hungry thousands now?

For now, consider these three words: "community" (he made them sit down); "commemorate" (he gave thanks); and "communion" (he revealed God's interactive presence in the mysteries of earth, sea, and sky). These words reflect the rhythms of any worshiping community centered in the sacraments. The church is gathered to be fed and then scattered to search for the lost, excluded, and hungry. Any congregation that ignores this rhythmical mandate misses badly the intent of Jesus's teachings. Later in this same chapter, Jesus upbraids several people who seem to have misunderstood the central point of the feeding miracle. "You are looking for me," he tells a group of followers, "not because you saw signs, but because you ate your fill of the loaves. Do not work for the food that perishes, but for the food that endures for eternal life, which the Son of Man will give you" (John 6:26-27). Jesus is concerned with feeding people, but he's even more concerned with nonperishable food, spiritual sustenance for the long road ahead.

It is here that the author of this gospel begins a rather jarring segue (for the balance of chapter 6) from the feeding miracle to an extended reflection on bread, body, flesh and blood, all of which, admittedly, sounds a bit like cannibalism to folk new to church life or returning after a lengthy absence. Sacramental life in church community requires a large leap of imagination, regardless of specific Christian tradition. The bread and wine received by communicants becomes something more than what they appear.

Kneeling at an altar, I swallow the sacrifice of Jesus and his new life, a different way of looking at and perceiving this world that normally invites hoarding of resources solely for me and mine. This meal, for centuries, reflects the paschal mystery of the Christian life. Embracing the sacrificial death of Jesus as the shape of one's own life brings meaning and purpose to solemn evening news that suggests only scarcity. Offering one's life for others in gospel mimicry of Jesus shapes and directs any chosen vocation with "food that endures for eternal life." Death is at work in this meal; ditto resurrection.

One important (and overlooked) element of baptism, at whatever age the sacrament occurs, is a radical joining of the baptized to the death and resurrection of Jesus (see Rom. 6:1–16). *Baptism is a death.* Those who are baptized have *already* died and need not fear some shadowy last day of breathing that lurks somewhere out in the future.[8] Some Christians make the sign of the cross over their bodies in worship and as a devotional practice throughout the week. This is not liturgical voodoo, even if some professional athletes make the sign seemingly invoking assistance for the next free throw or while on deck for their next at bat. The sign of the cross is a reminder of baptism, the shape of the Christian life. "For those who want to save their life will lose it, and those who lose their life for my sake will find it" (Matt. 16:25). This is the food (the radical sacrificial diet) that endures. Is this also a miracle? In my experience, yes, it is.

"I am the bread of life," says Jesus. "Whoever comes to me will never be hungry, and whoever believes in me will never be thirsty" (John 6:35). Jesus fed thousands on a beach, but the invitation following this miracle sign points to an even greater claim: abundance where all are potentially fed with his sacrificial life.

8. See Frank G. Honeycutt, *Death by Baptism: Sacramental Liberation in a Culture of Fear* (Minneapolis: Fortress, 2021).

*4. John 9:1–41: A Sign That Points to New Sight,
Challenging Blind Certainties*

Take a moment to read the next miracle in John's Gospel—another lengthy narrative with several distinct scenes that was used in the early centuries of the church to prepare adult candidates for baptism. Notice all of the skeptical questions surrounding a man (blind from birth) who suddenly sees when Jesus rubs mud in his eyes and tells him to wash in a nearby pool.

The questions land powerfully with my own general skepticism and perhaps yours. Well, "where is he?" (9:12) (a question posed by many of my skeptical friends who desire a little proof of Jesus's existence). "What do you say about him?" (9:17) "Is this your son . . . ? How then does he now see?" (9:19) "What did he do to you?" (9:26) "Are you trying to teach us," Mr. Whippersnapper? (9:34) So many questions in this miracle story. Also notice, not a soul in this cast of skeptical characters bothers to celebrate this man's good fortune.

Jesus clears his throat and spits a healthy glob onto the ground. Some see a connection here with the dust from which humans were first shaped (Gen. 2:7). Jesus bends down and makes mud. My mother tells me that I used to eat mud when I was a little boy. She always suspected there was some sort of mineral in the Tennessee clay across our back alley that I was not getting at the dinner table. This old reference to making mud makes me think of children and how free of guile and pretense they are, open to wonder and mystery. When I was a summer-camp counselor, the favorite day of the week for my fifth-grade guys was the rainy day where we were all given the green light to have mud battles, rolling around in the slop and muck with much laughter. Mud is a great leveler, stripping away the inflated sense of self-importance we all carry around as adults.

Spreading this muddy paste on the man's eyes, Jesus says, "Go, wash in the pool of Siloam." The name "Siloam" means "one who has been sent." The blind man who can remember nothing but darkness since birth maybe senses that this stranger, one who's just mysteriously entered his life, uninvited, has been sent by God. With the goop dripping from his eyes, he washes. And for the first time in his life, this man can see trees and clouds and the texture of his father's face. After the healing, Jesus vanishes. And then the interrogation begins—lots of skepticism, plenty of doubt.

Why is everyone so nervous? Why will no one celebrate this man's good fortune? First, the neighbors wonder whether this is truly the same guy who has for all these years been minding his tin-cup, guitar-playing business down at the five and dime. Some said, "Yes, it's the same guy." Others, "No, it's just somebody who's his spitting image." The once-blind man said, "Guys, hey, it's really me. Don't you know me?" I'm not sure anybody in the entire neighborhood ever really believes him.

Next, the local religious leaders get into the act. They call him downtown not once but twice and make him tell his story several more times. They take copious notes, add to a thick file, and shake their heads suspiciously. "Tell us again now what he did to you. Leave nothing out. Give us all the details." During the second interrogation, the once-blind man loses his patience and gets uppity with his religious superiors, maybe the same ministers he's admired all his life. And for that sassiness, he's driven out of the community.

The saddest part of this whole story, however, is when the parents of the blind man are called in to answer a few questions. "This is your son, right? Whom you *say* was born blind? Explain to us why he's now riding a bicycle all over town." The parents refuse to get involved. They claim that this man is indeed their son and confirm his blindness from birth, but they won't go out on a limb for him. "He's over twenty-one," they say. "Ask him yourself how all this happened, but please don't involve us." They are afraid. Thanks, Mom and Dad, for all your support.

What is it with these people? And please don't limit this question to the Jewish leaders who happen to populate this story. This old tale could easily be told on any religious group, folk who are absolutely certain that they have the corner on the truth—including, of course, Lutherans like me. The Pharisees ask, "Surely *we* are not blind, are we?" Jesus says, "Now that you say, 'We see,' your sin remains." It's weird, but *absolute certainty* often blinds me, potentially blinds anyone.

I love this old quotation from Paul Tournier, a Swiss psychologist whose influence spanned the third quarter of the twentieth century. "I have noticed more and more how dangerous it is for us to be right," he once said. "The most fruitful hours in life are those of humiliation when we see how wrong we are. As long as we zealously uphold a cause in which we know ourselves to be right, we remain inaccessible to anything new." A large part of what this story is about is the *blindness of certainty*, religious or otherwise.

We are a suspicious people here in America—suspicious of liberals, suspicious of conservatives. We often don't trust the wealthy and sometimes wonder about people on public assistance who we suspect are welfare cheats. We've been deceived so much and so regularly that we suspect just about everybody—often with good reason. So, it's easy to make close friends with people who echo our own beliefs, gathering in coalitions or clubs or over coffee to share our mutual suspicions about others who oppose us.

Over time, this creates enemies of change, constantly wondering about the motives, integrity, and honesty of others. It's a damaging way to live, to always be suspicious, in our national climate.

This story of the man born blind appears at least seven times in early-church catacomb art, most frequently illustrating Christian baptism. The church, then and now, invites a baptized Christian, over and again, to ask, What am I *still* blind to? What do I still refuse to see? My skeptical friends who've given up on church rightly see the blind disconnect between political partisanship in church life and the radical teachings of Jesus.

Jesus clears his throat and spits a healthy glob into the old dust. "Remember that you are dust, and to dust you shall return," the church is told each Ash Wednesday. "Go wash in the pool of Siloam," says the one sent into a suspicious world.

This story about blindness and sight is mostly a birth story. God's water breaks. We are born. We come up for air, dripping wet, able to see through the eyes of Christ for the first time, but hopefully not the last.

Surely we are not blind, are we?

This was the ironic question of ancient religious leaders. But maybe any of us, masters of suspicion, should let it hang there in our own lives for a while. Righteous certainty can cloud our vision, believer and skeptic alike. Jesus invites us to see clearly a new community of justice and peace. Is this a miracle? Given these weird times of deception, conspiracy theories, and the embrace of lying, I'd say so.

5. John 11:1–44: A Sign That Points to Liberation from Our Great Fear of Death

The fifth and final sign we'll tackle in John's Gospel seems, centrally, to be about the miraculous raising of a mummified dead guy, a family friend of Jesus named Lazarus whose grief-stricken sisters let the tardy miracle man have it when he shows up late for their brother's funeral. I suspect this story probably raises your skeptical radar more than any I've yet tackled. Again, the details (and there are many in this lengthy tale) matter mightily. I'll sift through several of them—Bibles open, please—and try to make the case for a miracle even greater than the resuscitation of a corpse.

Jesus seems to know this family better than most. Mary, Martha, and Lazarus have a history with the man—meals, implied previous conversations and offered hospitality, a long friendship. The town Bethany literally means "house of affliction."[9] Keep the name in mind as the story unfolds. It's only two miles from Jerusalem (11:18), site of a grisly crucifixion on the near horizon. The story addresses Jesus's rather odd response to affliction, coupled with a neighborly chorus (11:37) whose pointed chide suggests that his response to the illness of a friend is sorely lacking: "Could not he who opened the eyes of the blind man have kept this man from dying?" It's not a bad question, one raised consistently in my pastoral ministry by both skeptics within church walls and others determinedly unaffiliated. (Chapter 5 is entirely devoted to this theological quandary if you'd like to peek ahead a bit.)

Five odd details jump out in this long narrative, also used in the early centuries of the church in a protracted and unrushed period of baptismal preparation and reflection known as the catechumenate.[10] First, upon receiving a message from the sisters and learning of his friend's illness, Jesus says, reassuringly and with boundless confidence, "This illness does not lead to

9. The prefix "beth-" means "house of." "Bethlehem," incidentally, means "house of bread," a suggestive sacramental detail that Jesus was born in a town of many bakers.

10. The church-year season of Lent grew out of this pre-Easter period leading up to baptism.

death" (11:4). Since Lazarus does certifiably croak later on, one must conclude that Jesus was an underachiever in this particular prediction—he's divine *and* human, after all, claim the creeds—or something else entirely (recall John's delightful polyvalence) is going on. I vote for the latter, as you'll soon discover, but this air of confidence does serve to stir the pot a bit as the curtain rises on the story.

Imagine yourself in a hospital emergency room late one night with other family members. You're there because your brother has been wheeled in, bloodied and battered from a bad car accident on a nearby interstate. Around midnight, a doctor emerges from the "Personnel Only" double doors and reports that your beloved brother will make it through the emergency surgery. "Rest easy," says the comforting doctor, "some of you should go home and get some sleep." Relief, joy, thanksgiving. Two hours later, however, your brother takes a turn for the worse. By dawn, he'll be dead. Doctors are also human. Some prognoses are wrong. You know this, cognitively, reasonably. But your reaction to the doctor is not (cannot be) reasonable in the moment. Anger and grief are close cousins.

"This illness does not lead to death," Jesus says with confidence. One might ask, candidly, "Well, what in the hell does it lead to?" Keep this question in mind as the story unfolds.

Curious detail number 2: Jesus is late. Appallingly tardy. After hearing of the illness, Jesus "stayed two days longer in the place where he was" (11:6). No excuse is ever offered to these siblings whom Jesus loved (11:5). When Jesus (finally!) shows up, "Lazarus had already been in the tomb four days" (11:17).

Jesus was a true man of compassion. Even if you're new to the Bible, the evidence in this regard is immense. The sisters of Lazarus knew this, but the tardiness of Jesus frankly pisses them off. They meet the latecomer on the road, and both women are furious. Surely through clenched teeth, they hiss out the same hot words, "If you'd been here, pal, if you'd gotten off your lazy ass when you first heard the news, our beloved brother would still be alive" (11:21, 32; a rough F. G. H. translation).

I've been a pastor for a long time. Funerals are fraught with a variety of emotions very near the surface of any accompanying human interaction. I've seen mourners drunk, angry, regretful, resentful, fearful, and confused. All are understandable reactions. It's a tense time, even if the death is expected. Most families know this. All clergy expect such. What would not be tolerated in this emotional mix is tardiness, by either a seemingly uncaring family member or, God forbid, a pastor who decided to stay at the beach a few more days because the fish were biting. Let this detail also sit for a while. Jesus seems to be in no hurry to arrive and offer comfort and perhaps a bit of healing magic for a close family friend. I used to love Mighty Mouse, the cartoon rodent who swooped in with the theme song, "Here I Come to Save the Day." Jesus does not swoop in here, far from it. Why not?

Odd detail number 3: Jesus weeps in verse 35. That detail alone is not so weird. A good friend has just died. Jesus is overcome with emotion. Perhaps you'll never sign on with the possibility of biblical miracles, but maybe this side of Jesus appeals to you. Who wouldn't cry at the death of a good friend? I tear up at traffic lights, years after his funeral, upon thinking of a close hiking friend who died from brain cancer.

Jesus is crying here, however, from emotions other than grief alone. On either side of his tears (verses 33 and 38) is the curious phrase "greatly disturbed," which translates a Greek verb suggesting anger. Jesus is not only sad here. He's also a bit annoyed, ticked—a state of mind that carries over to details 4 and 5 in this odd tale of tardiness and testiness. He's rather terse with Martha (no. 4) at the tomb—Didn't I mention all this already, girl? (verse 40)—and then offers an impatient and pointed out-loud prayer (no. 5) "for the sake of the crowd standing here" (verse 42).

"The dunderheads," Jesus seems to be thinking, "they expect me to be some snappy miracle man or something." It's impossible to completely interpret tone and tenor in the Bible, but Jesus seems rather put out with those gathered around the tomb of Lazarus. A once-dead man does indeed eventually walk out of that tomb, but there's quite a bit of tension lingering in the air as the story ends.

"Unbind him," instructs Jesus, "let him go." Lazarus is sprung from the sadness of death, liberated from his grave bindings. A brother is restored to his sisters.

(Check out the lavish dinner in the next chapter and the extravagant and costly gift from a very grateful Mary.) By the end of this tomb tale, however, one must wonder who was really bound all along and by what?

Jesus will not be jerked around by death in this story. He absolutely saunters to the cemetery and seems to offer a classic misdiagnosis that instead eventually reveals the illness that paralyzes us more than death itself—that is, *our great fear of it*. Misunderstood by the sisters and the crowds ("do something, miracle man"), his weepy emotion is about far more than grief.

Yes, the raising of Lazarus was miraculous. But even more impressive for me is Jesus's calm, measured response to death as others are running about and losing their heads. There are worse things than death, this story seems to suggest. And what might that be? My own is the frenzied, fearful paralysis concerning that future day when I stop breathing—a foreboding reality for any of us that shapes all sorts of unhealthy and cautious behaviors on this side of the grave.

This fifth and final sign in John's Gospel liberates a follower of Christ to fully embrace, live out, and risk the implications of the previous four: a life filled with joy and ferment (water to wine); a life that trusts the forgiveness and acceptance of a fully exposed past (the woman at the well); a life lived in community where the hungry are fed (a meal for five thousand and more); a life where past certainties that block clear vision give way to new insights (the man blind from birth). Freed from the fear of death, one is also utterly free to live an unusual and altogether risky and sacrificial life, offered for the sake of others.

*

Okay, now that I've given you an abundance of Bible background on five miracles of Jesus and several spiffy maxims, I can hear you still asking, "Can't one live the exact same truth revealed here without signing on to mind-boggling paranormality? Why do the miracles themselves remotely matter to Christians (or anyone at all) in living a quality and even sacrificial life?" Both are fair questions.

In one of his short stories, fiction writer George Singleton has a character named Eddie who whimsically plays with one of Jesus's famous blessings (Matt. 5:5) until it comes out, "The bleak shall inherit some mirth."[11] The miracles I've described in John's Gospel serve as signs that joy and mirth, despite ample evidence to the contrary, accompany those who walk into tombs, deal with embarrassing pasts, and face hungers both real and metaphorical.

These miracles do not rid the world, once and for all, of any of the challenges that the characters in these stories face in spades—thirst, embarrassment, hunger, hypocrisy, and fear. But the stories do shape disciples who are formed to deal with and resist the soul-crunching reality of all five. The stories are like candles in a dark

11. George Singleton, "When Children Count," in *You Want More: Selected Stories* (Spartanburg, SC: Hub City, 2020), 93.

cave. They do not provide light all the way to the end of anyone's life path. Instead, these miraculous tales call forth trust to take the next steps, even mirthfully.

The next chapter will delve into several miracles that fall under a specific biblical genre—paranormal events that occur in nature. The chapter will be framed by my own travels by bicycle and trail, and specifically encounters with a good friend who died not long ago, unexpectedly. I suspect you'll discover that his lifelong questions about God—doubts that shaped countless letters between us over the years—find intersection with your own questions about the Christian faith.

3

Jesus and the Natural World

Then one day I was walking along Tinker Creek thinking of nothing at all and I saw the tree with the lights in it . . . grass that was wholly fire, utterly focused and utterly dreamed. It was less like seeing than like being for the first time seen, knocked breathless by a powerful glance.

—Annie Dillard

If we believe that writers are influenced by places as well as texts, it makes sense that a careful scholar, as a matter of credibility and authority, should check those sources, making use of what Simon Schama calls "the archive of the feet."

—Ian Marshall

Forty-five years ago, just out of college, I met an atheist at a summer camp in upstate South Carolina whose friendship would shape my theological formation and pastoral ministry more than any seminary professor I have ever had—which is saying a lot. I've been blessed with excellent teachers.[1]

My friend and I worked with profoundly mentally challenged children and adults and exchanged long letters for the next four decades. The letters often described why I believe in a loving God and why he could not. I use the word "atheist" to describe my friend, but it is not a title Andy ever embraced.

"I refuse to define myself in terms of God," he once wrote.

Andy consistently raised excellent questions in our exchanges and was honest (and loving) enough to probe my sometimes-flimsy arguments. "Is your God found only in sunsets and curly-headed babies," he once inquired at three o'clock in the morning as I rocked a disturbed and wailing child in a camp cabin, "or also

1. Portions of this introduction to chapter 3 (in slightly different form) are taken from my essay, "A Preacher's Skeptical Friend," *Living Lutheran*, September 2021, 30–32.

revealed in hurricanes?" It was not difficult to detect his meaning.

A longtime admirer of Albert Schweitzer, Andy was the most compassionate and gentle person I have ever known, and maybe the funniest. I once skipped matins, morning prayer, to write him from the seminary pecan grove before my next class (Lutheran Confessions) began at eleven. The first sentence of his reply letter, arriving two weeks later, read, "Quit skipping chapel, you son of a bitch."

He once sent us a "For a Special Minister and His Family" card at Christmas with this printed stock greeting:

> May God's richest blessings
> Be granted to you
> Not only at Christmas,
> But all the year through.

I found it in a shoebox the other day. The word "God's" was crossed out. An asterisk led to the bottom of the card and his bold handwriting: *misprint.

Dated February 28, 1993, and postmarked from West Forks, Maine, a letter from Andy arrived at our church parsonage in Virginia, responding to a long explanation of Lent that I'd offered, trying to help him understand the significance of the season for Christians:

> I very much enjoyed your last letter. Before I realized it, Ash Wednesday was over and I didn't get to smudge my forehead with Maine earth, so on Thursday I did the next best thing—I cursed God. I couldn't have

gotten to the Maine earth anyway as I have about 40 inches of snow on the ground and then I would have found the ground frozen and I would have had to chip some off and bring it in to thaw and I figured it just wasn't worth it to do something that Christians do. I tried to understand what you said about Lent and dying and Jesus and figure I didn't because I couldn't see any significance in it. I feel this in general—people get so wrapped up in myth and ceremony (be it political, patriotic, moral, religious) that they don't know their asshole from a hole in the ground. It is more important (and apparently enough) for people to have myths that embody their image of themselves than to actually *be* the embodiment. Our image of ourselves as a nation is kind, freedom-loving, and the fact that we are warlike in actuality is unimportant. And that has been a concern of mine with organized religion. The myth becomes more important than actually being.

In his fifties, Andy bought a Greyhound bus ticket after a long backpacking trip, returning to his cabin in Maine. Dog-tired, he stowed his pack in the luggage compartment under the bus, climbed the stairs, and settled into the last remaining seat on the back row.

His seatmate, recently released from prison, was a friendly and talkative person with a glass eye. The man would not let Andy sleep and kept flashing pictures of a partially clothed girlfriend waiting at his destination, revealing a good bit more than Andy cared to see. The man repeatedly removed the eye from its normal resting place and at one point reached over the seat in front of them, holding the eye between index finger and thumb, startling two young women with the words, "I can see you! I can see you!"

The bus driver pulled over, walked to the back, and threatened to throw both men off the bus. Andy was too tired to offer a defense.

I can see you.

*

Many people I've met in over thirty years as a parish pastor resemble a character in John Updike's novel, *In the Beauty of the Lilies*. After years of study, the Reverend Clarence Arthur Wilmot eventually concludes that "the God of the Pentateuch was an absurd bully, barbarically thundering through a cosmos entirely misconceived." Wilmot eventually leaves the church and ministry entirely, deciding to sell books of actual facts, encyclopedias, for a living. "Clarence's mind was like a many-legged, wingless insect that had long and tediously been struggling to climb up the walls of a slick-walled porcelain basin; and now a sudden impatient wash of water swept it down into the drain. *There is no God.*"[2]

My own relationship with God has certainly been challenged (even rocked) by friends like Andy who could clearly see shortcomings and even absurdities in my own faith life. Christians, of course, have their own set of theological challenges, notably the presence

2. John Updike, *In the Beauty of the Lilies* (New York: Knopf, 1996), 5-6.

of rampant, unjust suffering in the world and a God who seems silent in the face of it all, realities rightfully exposed by any clear-thinking nonbeliever.

Bald atheism has its own siren appeal. But those who give up God entirely are not off the hook. Given the abundance of intriguing and recurring profundities in the natural world, there's still quite a bit of head scratching and mystery even after removing God altogether from the creation equation, still a plethora of questions concerning how we and so much beauty and curiosity came to be. I suspect even my most skeptically dubious friends would pause over this observation offered by Patrick Glynn: "If the difference in mass between a proton and a neutron were not exactly as it is—roughly twice the mass of an electron—then all neutrons would have become protons or vice-versa. Say goodbye to chemistry as we know it, and to life."[3] To consistently fall back upon a position of complete randomness to explain our existence is, at the end of the day, not very satisfying (or persuasive) for me.

Atheists and believers need one another in lengthy and lasting friendship marked with deep listening and mutual respect, not with some covert agenda to convince the other of a particular position. The Holy Spirit, as I understand Christian theology, is the ultimate agent of conversion, should that eventually occur in someone's life.

3. Patrick Glynn, *God, the Evidence: The Reconciliation of Faith and Reason in a Postsecular World* (New York: Three Rivers, 1999), 29-30.

Andy died in September of 2020 in his sleep beside his faithful dog, Gandhi, at his off-the-grid homestead in northwestern Maine, only three weeks after a diagnosis of prolymphocytic leukemia. He was perhaps sicker than he knew or was willing to say.

The week he fell violently ill, Andy was doing one hundred pull-ups per day (a decades-long discipline) from a beam in his tightly insulated twelve-by-twelve-feet cabin with a small loft. The man was in fantastic physical shape. He backpacked the entire Appalachian Trail *five separate times*. Add in one through-hike of the Pacific Crest Trail (from Mexico to Canada) and most of the Continental Divide Trail. My diminutive friend (five feet five) logged well over fifteen thousand miles of unassisted backcountry trail hiking in his lifetime, not to mention a solo bicycling trip from North Carolina to Guatemala. He loved the natural world and its creatures, great and small, refusing to kill even the peskiest of insects.

Andy built the small Maine cabin himself near a reliable spring and often snowshoed during the winter (well before dawn) to his truck—parked at the closest cleared road over a mile away—and on to his job as a nurse in a residential facility near the Kennebec River. Walks in the snowy darkness (sometimes with moonlight) were among his favorite parts of the homesteading life.

I can see you. God, I'm convinced, brings surprising people into our lives, clearly seeing the ones we need the most. The Creator saw an unusual and delightful man whom I needed in Andy, an amazing agent of the holy. This book is dedicated to his memory, and this chap-

ter to those who made the Appalachian Trail possible.
I would have never hiked its length (2,190 miles) from
Maine to Georgia without Andy's influence. My pastoral
ministry would have been vastly different without the
questions he relentlessly and lovingly posed. He helped
shape more sermons, classes, and conversations with
Christian seekers than any friend I've ever had. I regret
that I never told him that, which would have undoubtedly amused him.

*

August 22, 1980
9:17 p.m.

Dear Cindy, . . . Andy's asleep right now and it's dark
and quiet except for two loud hikers in the lean-to
up the trail. We reached the top of Mount Katahdin
yesterday but only stayed for 30 minutes, part of a
long day that started at 5:30 a.m. and ended just before dark. We covered 19 miles in all. Baxter State
Park was full so we had to stay outside the park at a
campground along the trail. We left our packs in my
tent and hitched to the base of Katahdin to start the
day. It was 5 miles up a trail called The Knife Edge,
5 miles down the A. T. proper after reaching Baxter
Peak (elev. 5269), and then over 9 more miles on the
App Trail back to my tent and our packs. The first
day wasn't all that pleasant (except for tremendous
views on Katahdin), but couldn't be helped. Today
was better. My poor feet were in such bad shape that

Andy suggested we only go a short way—3.5 miles.
My blisters were no worse, so I was thankful for that.
A good supper of Mac & Cheese plus hot tea tasted
extraordinarily good. All for now. I love you, Frank

I hiked roughly half of the Appalachian Trail in
1980-1981—before marrying Cindy and entering seminary—and finished the trail at Springer Mountain,
Georgia, between the completion of my internship year
in Boone, North Carolina, and start of my senior year
in late summer of 1984. I walked three hundred miles
with Andy (essentially the state of Maine), five hundred
miles with Cindy (a good chunk of Pennsylvania and
Virginia), and over thirteen hundred miles alone, always southbound. Equipment was heavier back then.
My pack and ten days of food sometimes pushed sixty
pounds. I recall eating an entire package of Fig Newtons
only three miles out of Gorham, New Hampshire, and
the beginning of the White Mountains—a quick way to
lose a pound of weight from the overall load! The trail
was far less crowded in the early 1980s than today. Sometimes I'd go as long as four days without seeing another
soul. Only two thousand people or so had completed the
entire Appalachian Trail in 1984. (That number is now
much higher.)

No cell phones existed in the early 1980s, of course, or
any way to let family know of your safety. One had to use
pay phones in towns scheduled five to ten days apart. Mail
in trail towns with names like Rangeley, Delaware Water
Gap, Pearisburg, and Damascus became a major event of
anticipation assisted by unfailingly kind postal workers

on the lookout for hikers. Many letters awaited and sometimes boxes of supplies, and absolutely zero junk mail.

My hike took about six months altogether. Some hikers now complete the trail in less than one hundred days. The pace was perfect for me—time to look up wildflower names and linger over long views. I still think about the trail almost every day, easily the hardest physical and mental challenge in my adult life—long, relentless climbs and knee-pounding descents. The trail often gains one thousand feet of elevation (or more) in a single measured mile. Quite steep! The trail shaped my pastoral work, influenced how Cindy and I would introduce our three children to camping and hiking, and hovered in the margins of old stories in the Bible and how I interpreted tales of Jesus hiking on mountains and sailing across bodies of water, including storms.

*

At night in my tent several springs ago, during a week-long bicycle tour on the Blue Ridge Parkway with old friends, I reread with a headlamp parts of *Pilgrim at Tinker Creek*, Annie Dillard's wise year-long collection of observations along a small creek near Roanoke, her home at that time (1974) in Virginia.[4]

One of my favorite scenes in the book describes her childhood compulsion of hiding pennies at the base of sycamore trees, then drawing large arrows with sidewalk chalk from both directions. The arrows led to

4. Portions of this section are taken from my essay, "Automatically," *Living Lutheran*, October 2017, 5.

the coin, with statements like "SURPRISE AHEAD" or "MONEY THIS WAY." Dillard writes, "I was greatly excited at the thought of the first lucky passerby who would receive in this way, regardless of merit, a free gift from the universe."[5]

Early in Mark's Gospel, in several short teachings about the nature of God's present and coming kingdom, Jesus uses a variety of agricultural metaphors. One of my favorites describes how seeds sprout and grow in mystery, without much human assistance beyond the sowing (Mark 4:26-29). Jesus offers commentary on the process: "The earth produces of itself." Embedded in this phrase is an interesting Greek adjective: *automatē*, whence we get our English word "automatically."

According to Jesus, the coming kingdom is unconditionally inevitable. This parable is among the most radical in any gospel, for Jesus seems to announce the advent of the kingdom in its fullness regardless of whether we work toward such a reality—perhaps a rather serious blow to the human ego.

This is not to say Jesus feels humans are expendable, or that ambition and initiative are unimportant. He does, however, desire awareness of our relative place, inviting us over and again to consider how much of this life is sheer gift to be noticed and enjoyed. Someone once observed that authentic worship requires learning to pay attention—celebrating the joy of being alive on a planet filled with such prolific and mysterious diversity.

5. Annie Dillard, *Pilgrim at Tinker Creek* (New York: Bantam Books, 1974), 15.

One of the most powerful questions in the Bible comes early (Gen. 3:9), just after the first humans blow it in the garden. "Where are you?" God asks. This isn't a question of geographical location; the Lord knows their whereabouts. It's a question testing theological awareness.

Wonderful things happen in this old parable from Mark while the farmer is sound asleep, sawing logs, totally unable to make a difference or change the world. The seed sprouts and spreads while he does nothing to assist its growth. George MacDonald (1824-1905), a Scottish pastor and poet, once wrote, "Sleep is God's contrivance for giving us the help he cannot get into us when we are awake."

And lots of great things occur while we're sleeping, far beyond our ability to control or produce: planets and stars move across the night sky; mountain laurel bursts into bloom, resembling a hillful of snow; babies are conceived in a union never fully removed from mystery; schools of fish bore through tidal pools looking for a midnight snack; and the Spirit searches the heart of the guilty, ready to offer far more in grace than one could ever expect—*all after dark while we're snoozing.*

I suppose, given a piece of chalk, each of us might draw arrows to very different astonishing and grace-filled things. But being a disciple of Jesus will always mean retaining the excitement of children who urgently lead climate-controlled adults like me outside my shell (and outside, in fact) with an invitation to notice all the surprises hiding in plain view that God has authored around every bend in the trail. Perhaps that's why Jesus once declared the impossibility of entering the kingdom of God unless we all become like children.

*

Once upon a time, Jesus and one of his disciples had a little tiff about the direction that their ministry would take. Well, I take that back. It was a major tiff—shouting, name calling, pretty ugly stuff (see Matt. 16:21–26). This movement will be about self-denial and sacrifice, Jesus says.

Six days pass, and maybe Jesus senses he's been a little tough on the guys, a little terse. He decides to take three of them for a hike—time to get away, shake out the cobwebs, and reevaluate the ministry with no distractions, upon a mountain with God (Matt. 17:1).

Up they go, gaining elevation, scrambling over rocks, pausing for a sip from their Nalgene hiking bottles, maybe tossing back a handful of Mediterranean gorp. Not a word is recorded on the way up the mountain. Maybe there is some six-day-old tension still hanging in the air as Jesus and these three disciples climb the mountain.

Or maybe these three disciples (all fishermen please recall) are just sucking air on the way up and can't speak even if they want to. A footnote in my Bible reports that this is probably Mount Hermon, near Caesarea Philippi, about nine thousand feet high—significantly higher than any peak the Appalachian Trail crosses over. For fishermen, for guys used to coastal life, these disciples are not only winded but maybe also hallucinating about famous saints well before they reach the summit.

They all pile into the grassy meadow on top, wipe off the sweat, pass around water bottles, and finally notice Jesus standing on a nearby rise chatting with two, well, dead guys—and not just any two dead guys, but two Old Testament Hall of Famers whose busts were placed in perpetuity, so to speak, in the center-field honor of historic Judaism, Moses and Elijah.

Whatever else might be said about this odd, paranormal story known as the transfiguration of Jesus, it can be said with certainty that mountains—in the Bible and elsewhere—offer refreshing perspective on the troubling details of any life, a chance to reflect upon the finite number of days we're given and their purpose.

*

September 25–30, 1980
Near Mount Washington, New Hampshire

Dear Cindy, . . . My little radio told me early this morning that the rain would hold off until tonight. So, I decided to hike and made it here, an emergency shelter in Edmands Col that is wind, rain, and lightning proof, about three miles from Mt. Washington (elev 6288).[6] I'm far above timberline and it's terribly exciting to be here 'tho I can't see out of this little room for it has no windows. I'm not supposed to stay here except in case of emergency, but I didn't want to camp out in the open given the weather forecast. The

6. This emergency shelter has since been removed.

weather is getting chilly. Night before last at Zeta Pass it was 29 degrees.

(Next day). I could not leave this little shelter this morning—rain, fog, sleet, and wind like I've never seen. There are ten people here tonight, counting me. They're from a high school honors program and a pretty lively group. They gave me tomatoes, cheese, gorp, and raisins. Can't write anymore. I'm in this weird, contorted position with an elbow that's gone to sleep, so I will too. Hopefully the weather will be good tomorrow.

(9/27) . . . Finally left the shelter today about 1:45. The cloud cover lifted and produced a really beautiful day. It snowed last night, couldn't believe it! Everything around the shelter was frozen solid after a morning low of 25 degrees. Made it up and over Washington with about a quarter-inch of snow and ice with lots of wind. I wore just about every piece of warm gear I had. I'm now at Lake of the Clouds Hut in their refuge room as the actual hut is closed. So glad to see the cloud cover lift today.

(9/30) . . . I'm finally out of that unpredictable 13-mile stretch above timberline. Good hiking the last three days—10 ½ miles, 15 miles, and 11 miles. I'm camped about a mile from Franconia Notch if you have the map. Almost balmy today compared to the snow. Finally got to wear my shorts and t-shirt again. . . . Frank

Rereading my letters to Cindy over forty years later, I'm struck by how the Appalachian Trail offered so much time for me to think, reflect, and give thanks for the beauty of the mountains. Hiking gives one space and time to reflect upon why we're here and what might be our purpose in this life. "Jesus," writes Debie Thomas, "asks us to consider the lilies and behold the birds because every experience we have of the holy is grounded in the physical world we live in, the bodies we inhabit. God calls us to live an integrated life. . . . This integration isn't Christianity's side dish; it's the main course. It's why we're here: to notice, to reflect, to repair, and to multiply beauty."[7]

Peter and his companions are flummoxed, even angry, with Jesus's predictions concerning the arc of his life and death. And nor are they all that excited about such a cruciform shape of their own lives as his followers. A hike brings perspective. A hike surely reminds them of the long-term plan that God has in mind for the world, and the fleeting nature of their own lives in the meantime. A hike begins the process of new direction, crystallized purpose, and contact with a tradition much older than any of their objections or opinions.

It is very important for Peter, in particular, to see Jesus conversing with dead people who still spoke truth. There is a siren voice in any era that seduces us into thinking that ours is the most important moment human history has ever known.

Jesus, conversely, chats with the dead. He consults with those who had come before him. This is something

7. Debie Thomas, "Jesus the Poet," *Christian Century*, September 8, 2021, 35.

of what is meant when Christians say, "I believe in the communion of saints," in the third article of the Apostles' Creed. Our lives are shaped by the long gone. Or are they long gone? Jesus chats with two dead guys, which may sound strange. The point is that their memory, their witness, their teaching, and their legacy are still very much alive for him, shaping the arc of his own life and destiny. This mountain conversation leaves Jesus glowing from the inside out, as if he'd just swallowed a torch passed on to him from the distant past.

Peter doesn't quite get this, however, on the mountain, a reminder that a single hike is not some magical tonic. But Peter receives the best possible gift he could have ever received. Peter—in his chattiness to build something to commemorate the event—is interrupted.

"While he was still speaking, suddenly a bright cloud overshadowed them" (Matt. 17:5). We do not like to be interrupted. From a very young age, we are taught not to interrupt others. But Peter was interrupted that day right in the middle of his little mountain speech, and I have to think it was a profoundly important gift.

We are used to hearing our own voices—a steady, incessant stream of internal chatter that's difficult to silence. Some of it's judgmental. Some of it's vindictive. Some of it's downright angry. But it's a voice we carry around much of any day that gives shape to how we act and feel and behave toward others. We want to be heard and listened to. But sometimes our words are just plain wrong (or off) and we need to be interrupted. Peter is interrupted by a more important voice than his own. His confident chattiness, his certainty of being right from six days ago is finally silenced. He is overshadowed by God.

The word "overshadowed" is not a very common word in the Gospels. One time it's used is in the Christmas story. "The angel said to Mary, 'The Holy Spirit will come upon you, and the power of the Most High will overshadow you; therefore the child to be born will be called holy; he will be called Son of God'" (Luke 1:35). For birth to occur in the Christian tradition, we, too, must be overshadowed.

What, exactly, is overshadowed for Peter and company? Their agendas, their preferences, their chatty inner voice. All these things are interrupted, all overshadowed, by a surpassing voice. Hikes can have this effect on any of us. The wonder of the natural world elicits silence and awe in the wake of creation's vast mystery in a marvelously long view.

*

I think of a hike I once took with a now-deceased friend, Bill, many years ago in early February. Cindy dropped us off in the Nantahala Range in North Carolina on the Appalachian Trail. Our pickup point was seventy-five miles (eight days) away by trail. I cannot recall ever being quite so wet or cold with rain the entire week and temperatures that never rose above forty. You had to keep walking and keep eating to stay warm. We saw no other human beings the entire week. One night in a trailside shelter, a skunk (which felt like a warm cat) curled up on the end of my sleeping bag and innocently waddled away when a flashlight revealed its stripe.

On the seventh day, the weather broke and the temperatures dropped even further. We piled into another shelter. The moon came out, and I dove into my last dry gear to start dinner, waiting for the water to boil and pasta to cook. After several minutes of culinary distraction, it was startling to look up and see Bill standing on the lip of the shelter, bathed in moonlight, wearing nothing but his birthday suit. When questioned, he never turned around; he offered only two words. "I'm *drying*," he said. But for a moment, I mistook the words for what turned out to be a foreshadowing of the not too distant future: "I'm dying."

It was so cold on that mountain. "I'm drying," said my friend, wet with rain, sans clothing, a chilly reminder of his baptismal dousing. I thought I heard him say something else, and indeed, he would be dead much sooner than I knew.

How shall any of us live in a world filled with suffering? How shall we honor a life dependent upon the grace and love of those who've preceded us here? What shall be the shape of days that are limited and fleeting for any of us?

Jesus suggests that the true meaning of life will be days shaped by a cross. That is, days that are given away for others, sacrificially. This takes time for any of us to wrap our heads around. In my experience, hiking a mountain (requiring breath and breadth) is a recipe to help anyone see new directions.

*

November 10, 1980
Hudson River, New York

Cindy, . . . I crossed the Bear Mountain Bridge today after staying the night at Graymoor Monastery. The monks allow hikers to stay for free—food, shower, laundry, all at no charge. I felt so small walking across that river. Then, on top of Bear Mountain, I could see the New York City skyline! Could even make out the Empire State Building and the World Trade Center. Amazing. Some really nice long views from rocky ledges today. I love you. . . . Frank

*

Andy sent me a text message only three days before his death.

"You know, I'm baptized," he wrote. "My parents took care of that during my Methodist childhood. But if I wake up in your hoped-for heavenly place, I'll have to say, I didn't ask to come here." The man was dying and still making me laugh.

"All the way to heaven is heaven," said Saint Catherine of Siena (1347-1380). Annie Dillard expressed a similar idea as she took that piece of chalk as a child and hid coins for lucky passersby, heavenly gifts that are automatically strewn throughout the world. Too much of Christianity has historically focused upon who's in or out of heaven. Andy taught me where and how to look for the heavenly on the Appalachian Trail, and for that gift I'm grateful. For the balance of this chapter, I want to look at another long trip, this one via bicycle, and another old story about Jesus and the natural world. My story (and Jesus's) is about wind.

*

I'm grinding up a long climb on my bicycle to a place known as Chestoa View (elevation 4,090) on the Blue Ridge Parkway. Chestoa means "rabbit" in Cherokee. I keep looking for one, unsuccessfully, since leaving Famous Louise's Rockhouse Restaurant at lunch in Linville Falls, North Carolina, now regretting one too many hush puppies with the generous slab of catfish, mound of cole slaw, cup of green beans, piece of pecan pie, and four glasses of cold sweet tea with lemon. You burn a lot of calories on a loaded bicycle in the mid-May sun, but Lord have mercy. Too much sugar, too fast. It all felt good going down but not so great as I continue to climb up. This is one of those grueling parkway ascents with multiple false summits—things you don't notice in a car. An 8 percent grade works its way into any posterior, aging or otherwise, in a sweaty fashion that's hard to ignore.

No sign of the other guys, three ahead and three behind. I'm watching for cars in my small rearview mirror clamped to the left handlebar but eventually stop looking, as there's not much traffic out now anyway, with the threat of afternoon storms. It's overcast, and the wind from the west stiffens a bit with low rumbles of thunder in the distance. My red taillight is on. I pull off the Parkway into an overlook for a break, locate my yellow rain covers and preemptively slip them over the four panniers (two front, two rear). From the bottom of one of the panniers, I also fish my tiny lightweight umbrella (which has become a source of mockery over the years from purist pals) and make it more accessible in case I need to park the bike and wait out the rain in the woods. Let them laugh. I've hunkered under many a rhododendron bush with my minishelter and emerged drier than anyone, bowing, when the sun finally came out. I even did a little dance once in the right lane with my umbrella (à la Gene Kelly) in a torrential downpour that brought a bit of comic relief to a rather tense moment on another trip as we waited out the weather on the long climb from the James River up to Apple Orchard Mountain in Virginia.

I take in the long view from the overlook and think about the many spring week-long trips (now over thirty) with these guys that have been good for my pastoral soul. We call ourselves the Pannier People and have ridden the length of the parkway (and Skyline Drive) from Front Royal, Virginia, to Cherokee, North Carolina—some sections several times. Some of the guys are church members, but church talk is mostly off-limits. We do ponder odd Bible stories at night under the stars before entering our tents—marauding she-bears, talking donkeys, cooperative whales—and give thanks for the wonder of a world like ours spinning through a single galaxy. I read somewhere that nine galaxies exist for every human being (eight billion souls and counting) on the planet. That's a lot of galaxies.

Back on the bike, I instantly regret the anorak donned at the overlook. Two more false summits produce enough sweat that causes me to stop again and tuck the jacket under a bungee cord affixed to the rear rack.

I remember this climb from three Mays ago, recognizing a high bridge with a stream cascading far below, then passing red columbine clinging to a slope on the left and a forest filled with white trillium on the right, resembling scattered snow. The climb eases a bit. I slip the chain into another gear and know I'm getting close. The wind picks up with darkening skies. I pull into an almost-empty parking lot at the summit. My friend, Larry, is asleep on a picnic table, snoring softly. Three bikes are here. I don't see the other two, John and Ed. They're probably over at the viewing platform. The first drops of rain begin to fall.

I think of waking Larry but decide to throw my lightweight tarp over him instead. Some people can sleep through anything. He's the one who calls himself a Frisbeetarian, amusingly skeptical about God and Bible stories. Several years from now, the two of us will board bicycles together on the West Coast at Puget Sound and head east toward Maine for a cross-country adventure, across three major mountain ranges and fifteen states, that's currently only in our dreams.

*

The first part of the miracle story involving Jesus's mastery of wind and wave has always amused me. It's tempting to focus initially on divine control of nature, and we'll certainly get there. But surely Mark wants careful readers like us to notice these early details.

> A great windstorm arose, and the waves beat into the boat, so that the boat was already being swamped.

> But he was in the stern asleep on the cushion; and
> they woke him up and said to him, "Teacher, do you
> not care that we are perishing?" (Mark 4:37-38)

The story opens as night is falling. Jesus invites his disciples to board a sailing vessel and head to the other side of the sea. He doesn't mention the purpose of this nocturnal crossing. "Just get in the boat, guys," he seems to say. Jesus and his companions are constantly criss-crossing the sea from one side to another—thirteen times in the Four Gospels and five times in Mark alone. One side is Jewish, and the other is gentile. All the back-and-forth trips on water seem to suggest a subtle symbolic attempt to link the ethnically disparate sides of the sea, perhaps an early allusion to the core sacrament of baptism in the church's early ministry.

Wind is a normal companion on these crossings. There will always be resistance to attempts at reconciliation, racial or otherwise. (Peek ahead to chapter 5 in Mark and you'll discover a possessed man waiting on the far shore—more on this story and this phenomenon in the next chapter.) Then and now, there are forces in the world that seek to keep nations and ethnicities apart and separate. In Christ, allegiance to flag, race, and sexuality all take a baptismal back seat. "As many of you as were baptized into Christ have clothed yourselves with Christ. There is no longer Jew or Greek, there is no longer slave or free, there is no longer male and female; for all of you are one in Christ Jesus" (Gal. 3:27-28). The power and radical message of this oft-quoted verse should not be diminished by its familiarity. Jesus invited his disciples, flawed guys (like any of us) who would make up the early church, to board a boat at night and travel on an unclear mission to the other side—to "the other," the foreigner, the stranger, the enemy. There will be storms, wind, and plenty of resistance to such journeys. Serious conversations and reasons to resist such an embarkation in this or any century. Martin Luther, John Lewis, Harriet Tubman, Fannie Lou Hamer, Dietrich Bonhoeffer, and a host of others come to mind— much resistance to their minority vision, even from their friends.

All of this can be slowly sifted from this old miracle story. But I'm first amused by the cushion upon which Jesus rests his head; the little pillow Mark mentions even as the disciples yell in fear, receive a drenching from high waves, and begin frantic bailing. Jesus sleeps right through all of this rushing around and shouting. They actually have to wake the man up. I want to insert several sassy comments upon the lips of his chums who surely don't possess life jackets out there on the raging night sea. "Can we get anything else for you, Jesus? A glass of sherry perhaps? Maybe an Andes mint for your little pillow? Comfy, old bean? Cozy?" And then, "Don't you even notice that we're about to drown, Mr. Compassion? And why in the hell are we out here in the middle of the night anyway?"

*

*Bicycle Trip Day 1, May 25, 2018, Anacortes,
Washington, Puget Sound*

Loaded with camping gear, several days of food, dry
clothes, and an assortment of gadgets, two cyclists dip
rear wheels in water once fished and paddled by the Sno-
qualmie and Suquamish. Larry and I have planned for
months to arrive at this date, carefully considering the
weight and compressibility of our respective loads, ar-
ranged in four panniers and roughly balanced between
the front and rear of the bicycle.

Unlike the disciples who boarded the boat with Jesus,
we have detailed maps provided by a helpful group in Mis-
soula known as Adventure Cycling, folk who've stitched
together various and (relatively) safe routes to cross the
country via bicycle. Like those seafaring travelers, we're
heading for the "other side" of a vast and wide nation. We
chose the West Coast as a starting point to take advantage
of prevailing easterly wind but learn soon enough that
"the wind blows where it chooses" (John 3:8). It would
have been far easier that year to start on the East Coast.

In the next ten days, we'll cross the North Cascades,
climb five high passes (Rainy, Washington, Loup Loup,
Wauconda, and Sherman, the latter oddly named for
the famous Civil War general who spent some time in
the region), scream down the backside of each pass in
rapid descent, cycle past melting snowpack on scenic
Highway 20, pass through abundant cherry orchards,
and encounter more waterfalls than I've ever seen in ten
days, bringing us through the panhandle of Idaho to the
Montana state line.

Larry is carrying bear spray, just in case. We meet Warren, of the Kalispel Reservation, a cyclist and very funny man who's been hit twice by cars and still rides daily. He points us to Sunday brunch in Usk, Washington, across the wide and beautiful Pend Oreille River. Evan and Sandy, the proprietors, tell us that the bar in the diner floated downriver to Usk over a century ago. I wonder whether the disciples desired a bar on board that night all those years ago.

*

Storms at sea in the Gospels always reveal something unexpected about Jesus, and they reveal something quite predictable about reluctant followers like me. The chaos of the storm flushes out an ancient fear of sinister forces beyond anyone's control. Fear of the source of these unleashed forces has perhaps changed, but I've been caught in several storms that reminded me of the utter powerlessness and human inability to control outcomes, particularly a storm I recall in the Roan Mountain Highlands of Tennessee with a dozen young backpackers where we got caught on the high open Balds with crashing lightning and thunder that was directly on top of us with absolutely nowhere to hide. It was terrifying and perhaps the most afraid I've been in all my backpacking trips. It's impossible to engage in civil discourse with certain parts of nature. Rattlesnakes and lightning, among other phenomena, are not open to rational reason. You duck or run and get out of the way.

Jesus snores right through this intense, unmanageable storm. Once the man has rubbed the sleep out of his eyes, his frantic disciples ask, "Teacher, do you not care that we are perishing?" There's quite a bit loaded into that pointed question. It raises similar concerns to those posed by Lazarus's neighbors: "Could not he who opened the eyes of the blind man have kept this man from dying?" (John 11:37). *Do your thing, Jesus. Wiggle your divine nose. Get us out of this. You've got it in you, do something.*

Jesus will silence the storm, but there is something about his calm and rather surreal demeanor in the midst of this wild weather that Mark wants the early church (and latter-day disciples) to notice. The Gospels were initially written for Christian communities. The oral nature of the telling of the stories (before they were gathered and written down) shaped the theology and community concerns that brought the gospel into its present form. The nuances of the stories include details still sending messages to Christian communities that would eventually form centuries after the stories were first told, details that speak to worried and timid disciples like me, facing my own storms and sea-change crossings.

My close friend and hiking partner, Bill, whose nude moonlit "drying" on the trail I misheard for another word that night so long ago, indeed died after a long bout with brain cancer. He was about my age at the time with two young daughters and a great marriage. His death really shook me. I deal with death a lot in my profession, but his passing left me reeling and wavering back and forth between depression and anger. I remember stopping at traffic lights and breaking into tears. I talked with Bill's wife, Marty, not long after his funeral. "You know," she said, shaking her head in wonder, "he never complained about his illness. Never a single time. Not even privately with me, when the two of us were alone. He knew there was something else ahead." I've never forgotten those words that came to me like the ringing of a loud bell of recognition.

Jesus slept in the middle of a bad storm not because he was tired on that wild and windy night but because he was utterly confident in the presence of God, no matter what might occur.

*

Bicycle Trip Day 17, June 10, 2018, Glacier National Park

Larry and I wake up in the Halfway Hotel near Essex, Montana, along the south border of the park, bikes parked at the end of our beds. The wind is howling. Rain pours down in sheets. We'll do only thirty miles today, partly because of a late start in hopes that the weather will break. It doesn't.

I'm climbing toward Marias Pass (elevation 5,213) on Highway 2 in full rain gear—a light blue jacket with waterproof pants and bright yellow rain covers for the four panniers. My sleeping bag and tent are protected and lashed onto the rear rack. It's about forty degrees, and the temperature is dropping as we climb. Logging trucks blow past and shower us with road spray. My fingers and toes are freezing. After a few miles, I see a light in a camp office off to the right, pull in, and ask the woman at the counter if I can just stand in the heat of the place a few minutes. Her name (I learn) is Connie. She and her husband have welcomed RVs for national park adventures for almost two decades after moving here from the Midwest. I can tell that Connie doesn't trust me or Larry at first. We look disheveled and a little crazy, wet as rats. We tell her our story and offer a few details about our respective vocations. She warms up to us. We thaw out in general.

"Well, why are you doing this anyway?" she wants to know. "Why are you out here in such weather?" I briefly think of Jesus and his companions out in that boat, who cross a wide sea for no stated good reason on God's green earth, and the resistance they faced in wind and rain getting to the other side. We take a picture of Connie, our road angel, before departing. She's grinning by now. Before heading outside to our bikes, I think to ask her whether she knows the temperature. "Thirty-four," she says. "Be careful up on the pass."

It's snowing steadily when we reach the top, a long meadow. The snow's not sticking to anything but still hard enough to make a crazy June video with my phone, as I whoop it up. We descend carefully into East Glacier, the snow changing back to rain, and find another cheap hotel for the night. My fingers are absolutely numb. We shower and drink a half gallon of hot coffee between us at a nearby diner. The rain finally stops near dusk.

The wind, however, blows like I've never heard it before or since. We hear it all night. Tomorrow, with blue skies, an incredible tailwind will blow us 116 miles across Montana with very little effort, our longest mileage day for the whole trip. Larry passes his bear spray off to a westbound cyclist, Pat, battling the wind we're presently enjoying. We're about a week from North Dakota. Today will be our last true tailwind until day 62 at Lake Erie. Montana is stunningly beautiful, over six hundred miles wide, often with open vistas, a heavenly context for the serious cyclist. But Lord, have mercy—the wind. "Awe" is the right word for Montana weather.

*

"Do you not care that we are perishing?"

"Care" is a word that carries a great deal of emotional freight in movie narratives, novel plots, and a variety of relationships. "We're the Church That Cares" is a frequent motto on roadside signboards. Of course, Jesus cared about people. Stories of his caring fill the Four Gospels. Once the fearful twelve in that boat reach shore, they'll surely agree that Jesus is not on trial for an absence of care since they've met the man.

But Jesus consistently redefines the word in his relationship with people facing wind, suffering, and fear. He silences wind and wave in this old miracle story, and I suspect that also (at least temporarily) silenced the criticism from his twelve companions. "They were filled with great awe" (4:41). This nature miracle will inspire future prayers and hymns from many folk facing perils at sea, and also create doubts in a variety of skeptical imaginations concerning whether the miracle really happened. Let's return to my point about the origins of the Gospels: *Why was this story repeatedly told?* Was it to elicit awe and wonder and command respect for the new miracle man in town? Or, for another reason?

The real miracle in this old story may be hiding a bit. Jesus does indeed perform a nature miracle that truly inspires in all its power and profundity. But add together his casual lack of worry for the storm (a posture that lets him sleep through most of it) and the clear tension in the boat after the storm is over: "Why are you afraid? Have you still no faith?"

Jesus's main concern (even more than the storm itself!) seems to be *how* his followers will handle the storms and strong wind that come to any of us. A large part of the church's early mission was to form disciples in a meaty (and lengthy) educational process leading to baptism, a death (see Rom. 6:3–14) in Christ leading to a life free from fear. Although this ancient process can still be experienced in some congregational settings, many baptisms these days are rather rushed in the name of adding people to the church rolls. In baptism, however, there is always something at stake. The great fear of death and various ways anyone tries to stave it off is replaced by going ahead and dying in Christ.

In this old story, Jesus seems to be less interested in protecting disciples from mishap and more interested in their faith during storms that will surely come. Two chapters later, in another windstorm on the sea, Jesus comes out to his friends in a story of miraculous buoyancy and "intended to pass them by" (Mark 6:48) until their terrified cries beckon him into the boat. This is an exceedingly odd detail (leaving them alone on rough seas) until it's coupled with the previous story.

Jesus doesn't seem all that interested that disciples have faith *in* him to swoop down and miraculously fix everything. His exceeding hope and concern is that disciples will have the faith *of* Jesus in whatever storms that may come. Then and now, forming such disciples who are capable of withstanding any sort of wind is a miracle in its own right.

*

Bicycle Trip Day 52, July 15, 2018, Wenona, Illinois

We've generally been following the mighty Mississippi River south from Minnesota for several days with memorable camping and swimming spots. We just enjoyed a lovely three-night rest break in historic Muscatine, Iowa, with Jean and Cindy, our understanding wives, where we had great views right on the river in a brand-new hotel, the Merrill, whose fourth floor allowed for tug and barge sightings. Muscatine was once known for its massive pearl button industry, ingenious garment fasteners manufactured from abundant freshwater mussel shells harvested from the river.

Jean and Cindy drove two days to meet us in Muscatine—a joyous and long anticipated reunion. We consumed a lot of great food with long romantic walks all through the small city. Eastern Iowa near the river is not flat; it has plenty of hilly and high bluffs with tough climbs. It's been good to stretch our cycling legs for a few days.

Larry and I say goodbye, boarding saddles with delightfully rested posteriors. The Maine coast is about a month away. We cross the river into Illinois and angle northeast toward Cleveland, Buffalo (cities we'll eventually pass through), and the Great Lakes of Erie and Ontario.

I've lost count of all the great small-town diners like this one we're presently enjoying in Wenona (population 974), with its simple menu, great food, and local high school sports stars on two walls. We've been directed to the diner by a town resident named Matt, a friendly local first responder who also showed us the shower and camping area just for cyclists in a park a few blocks from here.

Matt lives near the park and comes over and talks later that evening after our tents are up. We sit on benches, watch several kids on nearby swings, and share details about our work lives and families as the sun sets. He's a great guy, easy to talk to, forthcoming in conversation, like so many others we've met this summer. Something about a bicycle instills trust. Fireflies start to come out. There's a bit of comfortable silence that Matt eventually breaks.

"This reminds me of an evening three years ago when I got a call about a wreck just outside of town. I was the first EMT to arrive. Just a single car, overturned, an old Impala that looked a lot like my son's vehicle." More silence. "I walked over to the edge of the corn row and knelt beside the body, which was not moving and thrown clear of the accident. It was him, my son. Gone, just like that."

Larry and I listen, stunned. We've talked for half an hour. Matt is so centered and confident describing this tragedy, full of enviable peace in an agonizing family storm that surely still rages at times. I pray for Matt for several days, heading east, not that far south of Chicago. Lots of time to wonder about this life while riding a bicycle eight hours a day. I regret something I didn't ask him in the darkness that night. Matt is a Christian and possesses, I could tell, a gift that's often so fleeting for me, even as a pastor. I wished I'd asked him how he now prayed and how he eventually found such peace in his life.

*

The two nature miracles we've been examining—the transfiguration story on a tall mountain and crossing a windy sea during a storm toward an unknown "other side"—possess several commonalities for sometimes skeptical people like me.

Climbing a high mountain always offers me plenty of perspective concerning place and time, geology and cosmology, destiny and chance. "Where are you?" God once asked the Bible's first humans after their famous slipup in the ancient garden (Gen. 3:9). God knew their geographical location, of course. This is a question that invites any of us to take stock, examine purpose, and ponder identity. Where am I indeed? Mountains invite a slow percolation of this question into even the most jaded heart. We need the long view to help decide what's next.

Jesus sensed it was time to get away and climb a mountain with his friends who would eventually help shape the early church. The fact that *any of us* exist in this world is rather miraculous and mysterious. The fact that a *genetically unique* person like you or me exists is enough to take anyone's breath away. Humans are the product of generations of encounters, choices, conversations, and seemingly chance intersections. Mountains invite such reflection.

The past is peeled back on that mountain, and Jesus chats with two dead people who are very much alive to him and continue to shape and guide him, who offer courage to continue with a life offered in sacrifice for others. The disciples on that mountain are indeed overshadowed by something far greater than their own brief histories. Any hike offers similar perspective as we ponder where we've come from and where we're going, as we listen for the stories of those who've come before us who cheer us on and further on. The truths we learn from mountains allow us to board many boats in this life with predictably choppy seas. To cross over, it's necessary to rely on a host of others who've preceded us.

Pastor and writer Lillian Daniel describes a woman in her congregation who suffered a stroke affecting her speech, which was gradually returning after much therapy.

> The last thing to come is our names. Church people visit her, and she can speak to us in ways that indicate she knows exactly who we are, and has known us for years, but she cannot speak anybody's name. Instead she pulls out the church photo directory. . . . When one of us from the church walks in to see the

woman whose speech is failing her, she waves the sacred church photo directory at us, as if to say that she does not know our names, but she knows the way in which we are all related.[8]

As one enters its stories over time and with ponderous frequency, the Bible works something like that church pictorial directory. The narratives, names, and acts of daring therein give me the courage to take the next step into the future. Jesus was so familiar with the heroes of Israel's past that a couple of them sprang out of the photo directory, so to speak, and onto the mountain to help him face what was coming in Jerusalem. I've no doubt that they (and many others) also gave him confidence to sleep peacefully in the midst of any storm he may have faced on the way. Jesus was so conversant with the tradition that the past shaped his present and future. The veil separating moments in time was lifted. Jesus could see clearly to the other side with a pictorial directory of faces and stories, shaking the directory at death itself.

The nature miracles were told and retold to shape and create disciples for whom fear did not have the last say, disciples capable of following Jesus daringly and sacrificially into the future, to and through various crosses—a central purpose of what would become the church.

8. Lillian Daniel and Martin Copenhaver, *This Odd and Wondrous Calling: The Public and Private Lives of Two Ministers* (Grand Rapids, Eerdmans, 2009), 3-4.

*

*Bicycle Trip Day 72, August 4, 2018, Near Mount
Moosilauke, New Hampshire*

In the last week, Larry and I have made a quick junket
into Canada (dazzled by Niagara Falls, even with all the
tourists), passed back into the United States among a sea
of cars at the border crossing station, ridden about one
hundred miles of the Erie Canalway Trail (including a
clandestine skinny-dip in the famous waterway on the
anniversary of my baptism, July 28), passed through
historic Ticonderoga and into New England via a short
ferry ride across Lake Champlain, and began some
of the last serious climbs of the trip in the Green and
White Mountains of Vermont and New Hampshire.
Andy will pick us up in Bar Harbor in five days where
front wheels will be dipped into the Atlantic, complet-
ing the seventy-seven-day crossing covering forty-two
hundred miles. We'll drop Larry at the Bangor airport
after shipping our bikes home. I'll spend four days with
Andy at his homestead near the Kennebec River.

I'm presently taking a break at the Appalachian Trail
crossing on Highway 112 before we descend steeply into
North Woodstock, New Hampshire, for the night.
Mount Moosilauke (elevation 4,802) is visible above
timberline on this clear day. Larry arrives and finds me
crying beside the trail sign with an odd mixture of joy
and release. I don't have a good explanation except that
this very spot links two long and epic trips almost forty
years apart. I walk across the road and follow the Appa-

lachian Trail for a few minutes toward the mountain, thinking of the guy I once was, trekking through here with a heavy (compared to today's ultralight gear) dark green Camp Trails backpack.

It's difficult to describe how this very spot spiritually connects a young man in his twenties before entering seminary with a retired pastor in his early sixties. How much has occurred and changed in between. A long west-east crossing linked with a long north-south so-journ. Larry gives me plenty of time to look around. We climb aboard the bikes and fly down the mountain at top speed, descending about fifteen hundred feet into town, the cyclist taking up the rear laughing loudly through tears like a Maine loon.

*

In the novel *Cold Mountain*, there is a beautiful exchange between the two central female characters. Ruby, with plenty of experience, has just arrived on a western North Carolina farm during the Civil War to help out Ada, who is a novice to mountain life and ways of the wild. One day, Ruby coyly asks Ada to ponder any hunches she might have about why sumac and dogwood turn color so early, in advance of the other trees, almost a full month ahead. Ada is flummoxed. "Chance?"

After noting that both trees are full of ripe berries in early fall, Ruby presses a bit further. "What else is happening that might bear on the subject?"

Birds were moving, "Enough to make you dizzy at the numbers of them." Ruby then notes how "green and alike" all the trees must look to passing birds. "They don't know these woods. They don't know where a particular food might live."

Ruby suggests there is a design to early color change. "Dogwood and sumac maybe turn red to say *eat* to hungry stranger birds."

Ada thinks on this information and says, "You seem to suppose that a dogwood might have a plan in this."

"Well, maybe they do," says Ruby.[9]

It's a rather staggering thing to believe that God is everywhere, omnipresent—as close as our next breath, and as distant as the stars. Given the world's wide and historic suffering, the siren call of atheism indeed has a certain appeal. Any serious Christian will confess that it's difficult at times to maintain faith in a world such as ours. But I think it's also hard to maintain unbelief in anything at all. It's hard to explain away the existence of leopards and coyotes and trout and the color purple as purely accidental and random. Theists have their own set of befuddling challenges. But so do atheists. My most skeptical friends often confess they're not quite off the hook concerning the mysteries of this life when they choose to give up God. Larry, my cycling pal, read this chapter and pushed back a bit on that idea in a friendly way, offering this interesting response: "It seems to me that the core difference in this regard between people like you and people like me is that you notice the infinite mysteries of life and want (or need) to have an explanation for them, to ascribe *intention* to the miracle of life,

9. Adapted from Charles Frazier, *Cold Mountain* (New York: Atlantic Monthly, 1997), 107.

so you conclude (that is, you have *faith*) that something called God is responsible for the mysteries. For me, the fact that there ARE infinite mysteries IS GOD! I don't ascribe intention to explain why there is being; I'm just in profound wonder that there is."

*

I've always been intrigued by how one of the central characters of the Bible experienced an abrupt transformation concerning where to experience God in his life.

> In the year that King Uzziah died, I saw the Lord sitting on a throne, high and lofty; and the hem of his robe filled the temple. Seraphs were in attendance above him; each had six wings. . . . And one called to another and said, "Holy, holy holy is the LORD of hosts; the whole earth is full of his glory." The pivots on the thresholds shook at the voices of those who called, and the house filled with smoke. And I said, "Woe is me! I am lost, for I am a man of unclean lips, and I live among a people of unclean lips; yet my eyes have seen the King, the LORD of hosts!" (Isa. 6:1–5)

In the year 742 BCE, the year of King Uzziah's death, Isaiah decided he would head down to the temple for worship in downtown Jerusalem with his family. He was married and had kids, responsibilities. On every Sabbath, like clockwork, he worshiped God in liturgical routine. He got through the first hymn okay that morning, and the lead musician was just getting ready to lead the congregation in the appointed psalm of the day when Isaiah saw and heard something that changed his life.

One might conclude that actually seeing God is what changed Isaiah's life and made him a prophet. Or, perhaps it was those six-winged celestial visitors that made him swoon. I think, however, that Isaiah is overcome by *the words of the song* the seraphim are singing. "Holy, holy, holy is the Lord of hosts; the whole earth is full of God's glory."

The entire earth is full of divine glory. As long as God is kept corralled in the temple, then Isaiah could effectively manage, domesticate, and tolerate the divine in a guy's life who had better things to do. It was only an hour a week after all. God could be kept on the margins, at a safe distance, trotted out when needed.

But what Isaiah saw and heard changed everything that day. Isaiah experienced just the *hem* of God's robe (6:1) utterly filling the worship space. The light bulb in the soon-to-be prophet's head was timed with his "woe is me" confession. "If just a corner of the divine robe fills this place," he must have thought, "then the rest of God is spilling into my tomorrow, my work week, my whole life."

Isaiah realizes that there's no setting in his coming days where God *isn't*. This is not such good news for Isaiah, at least not initially. He was used to keeping God in a convenient compartment, confined to a certain time of the week. But it was indeed the very best news he could have possibly heard.

"For God so loved the world" would be written centuries later by a gospel writer smitten with the life and death of Jesus and his saving work (John 3:16). But there is a connection in this famous verse to Isaiah's Sabbath-morning realization. The Greek word for "world" here is *kosmos*. God's love and concern is vast, the divine gaze as close as those trillium at Chestoa View and as distant as those recent glimpses through the James Webb Space Telescope.

*

My friend Andy died unexpectedly at his little cabin in Maine only two years after he met me and Larry at the conclusion of our bicycle trip on the Atlantic coast. Perhaps surprisingly for someone who once declared he "wanted to chase God down with a pitchfork," Andy taught me to expand my vision concerning where to look for the holy in this life—to get outside a church building and find perspective concerning life's profundities with the long view (even beyond the fear of death) coupled with the nearby gaze to shape tomorrow's next steps toward justice and peace. I miss Andy, forever grateful for his unique friendship.

The nature miracles in the Gospels, from mountain climbs to windy sea crossings, teach us to look for the miraculous in a variety of places. If just the hem of God's robe filled the temple, a sliver of the divine slip, there's a heck of a lot of the Lord's presence out there waiting to be experienced and discovered, shaping our various sacrificial vocations to help heal a broken world, and assisting ponderous disciples in making sense of the resistant wind keeping us from new shores.

In the next chapter, I want to take a closer look at this resistant wind and the dark challenges often facing any of us upon descending the exhilaration of a mountain—malevolent spiritual forces that attempt to derail the mission of inclusion and love to which the baptized are called. The church has long referred to this force by a variety of names: Satan, Lucifer, Beelzebul. Buckle your safety belts as we switch gears a bit and together examine an area of the Bible where skepticism perhaps offers its strongest catcalls of doubt—the strange New Testament world of the demonic and how Jesus miraculously confronts evil, then and now.

4

Jesus and the Demonic

I'd love to have a Christianity full of rainbows and daisies, full of love and inclusion. But there are forces working against love and inclusion in the world, and some of those forces are at work in my own heart and mind.

—Richard Beck

Put on the whole armor of God, so that you may be able to stand against the wiles of the devil. For our struggle is not against enemies of blood and flesh, but against the rulers, against the authorities, against the cosmic powers of this present darkness, against the spiritual forces of evil in the heavenly places.

—Ephesians 6:11–12

Forty years ago in seminary, I had a wonderful and witty teacher for my introductory course in theology. Dr. Michael Root was about a decade older than most of us, had a great and infectious laugh, and always started class right on time with the same four fast words: "Questions about the reading?"

Lord, have mercy, that man assigned *a lot* of reading and expected you to be ready when the bell rang, never handing us easy answers to our most pressing questions, wanting us instead to think and struggle. And for that I'm profoundly grateful. Future sermons or classes I planned would be marked with some open-ended idea or question that would hopefully stick with church members beyond our time together that day, inviting them to do their own homework and thinking on the matter along with me. Dr. Root had a lot to do with my developing preaching and writing style.

After my classmates departed one Monday morning, I sidled up to Dr. Root, following his lecture on baptism with a question that I was embarrassed to ask in class. Like several other denominational traditions, there's a section in the Lutheran baptism liturgy where the pastor asks candidates (or their parents) to "renounce all the forces of evil, the devil, and all his empty promises."

It's a rather heavy question posed to a young mother or father holding their beautiful and sometimes squirming child and perhaps thinking mostly about lunch later on with all the friends and family present for the happy occasion. And it's also a startling question posed to an adult of any age coming forth to join the church via this ancient and watery welcome into a new community of grace. In the early church, this renunciation of evil was a much more protracted period of time covering several weeks. Sometimes adult candidates were baptized just before dawn on Easter Sunday and were instructed to actually spit toward the western darkness, renouncing Satan, before turning to the eastern rising sun, doused into a new life.

Either way (a brief or lengthy renunciation) seemed like so much voodoo to me. Back then I was, at best, rather agnostic about the existence of the devil. Like most of my peers, I'd seen the exorcism movies of my era, saw Linda Blair's head spin around with accompanying satanic vomit, and was predictably spooked for a bit. But *believe* in the existence of the devil and evil forces? Come on.

I explained my dilemma to Dr. Root that Monday morning. "Do I *really* have to say that part about the devil? I'm pretty sure I don't even believe in his or her existence," smiling at my cleverness. "Would the baptism be any less efficacious if I just left those words out? How can I preside at anyone's baptism and say all that with a straight face?"

Just the two of us were standing there. He looked at me with direct and rather serious eye contact and let a

123

good bit of silence hang in the air before finally responding. And his answer wasn't even really an answer at all, even though I've never forgotten it.

"Spend twenty years in parish ministry," he said, pausing. "Then come back and ask me this question again."

I've never had to.

*

"Satan" and "Mephistopheles" are found in the legend of Faust, who made a regrettable deal with the devil. "Old Scratch" is likely from the Middle English word "scrat," the name of a demonic goblin, and is a popular moniker for the devil in the southern United States during the early 1900s and at present among certain prison inmates.[1] "Beelzebul" (Matt. 12:27 and other biblical citations) literally means "lord of the flies." "Lucifer" (literally, "one who bears light") is an ironic and curious title for one who slyly leads others into darkness, who often masquerades as good.

And my personal favorite is "the father of lies" (John 8:44), a single biblical instance found in a book that mentions the word "true" or "truth" over forty times and describes the very purpose of Jesus thus: "For this I was born, and for this I came into the world, to testify to the truth" (John 18:37). Please read that verse again, slowly.

---

1. See Richard Beck, *Reviving Old Scratch: Demons and the Devil for Doubters and the Disenchanted* (Minneapolis: Fortress, 2016), xiii–xiv.

Jesus spoke these words in front of a Roman judge, Pontius Pilate, who eventually signed off on his death sentence and famously replied, "What is truth?" (John 18:38), which is stunningly pertinent these days in America with an electorate enamored with politicians who chronically lie or stretch truth to the point of disappearance.

"If you continue in my word," Jesus says to his followers, "you are truly my disciples; and you will know the truth, and the truth will make you free" (John 8:31-32). Flannery O'Connor, the Georgia fiction writer who died in 1964, is often credited for this classic paraphrase: "The truth shall make you odd." How has such a large chunk of the nation become willing accomplices to an avalanche of deception, conspiracy theories, and downright fabrication? Simply telling the truth has indeed become rather odd and out of step.

Factor in the bald reality that *Christians* in America have enabled and voted for this behavior in electing a chronic and lifelong liar in what amounted to a Faustian and transactional deal with the devil, all the while ignoring clear Christian attributes ("fruit") of the spirit such as love, joy, peace, patience, kindness, gentleness, and self-control (Gal. 5:22-23). Various parishioners in churches of my acquaintance have told me that they "held their nose and voted for someone who could stack the court with judges of [their] liking."

Regardless of legitimate convictions inviting important dialogue on a variety of social issues, this is a dangerous dance of transaction with consequences as old as Eden (Gen. 3:1-7), complete with ancient *Let's*

Make a Deal lies mouthed by a deceptive and beguiling serpent. The national church, already reeling from significant membership loss over the last forty years, will certainly be affected by such religious hypocrisy, especially in trying to reach young people like my children (and their friends) who sense a wide and palpable disconnect between the compelling ministry of Jesus and those whom so many church people have chosen to elect. Lying is now presumably considered an acceptable political stance by many Christians if it leads to certain righteous outcomes, the end justifying practically any means. They may as well be saying, "I'm okay with a valueless, amoral, unprincipled bully to champion and fight for my holy values, morals and principles."

On sabbatical several years ago, while writing a book about pastoral truth-telling and the great need for such in parish life regardless of cost or fallout,[2] I ran across an intriguing idea about lying authored by Sissela Bok, an ethicist and philosopher. "If, like truth, the lie had but one face," she writes, "we would be on better terms. For we would accept as certain the opposite of what the liar would say. But the reverse of truth has a hundred thousand faces and an infinite field."[3] Bok would undoubtedly agree with this wry statement often attributed to

2. Frank G. Honeycutt, *The Truth Shall Make You Odd: Speaking with Pastoral Integrity in Awkward Situations* (Grand Rapids: Brazos, 2011).

3. Sissela Bok, *Lying: Moral Choice in Public and Private Life* (New York: Pantheon Books, 1978), 4.

Mark Twain: "A lie can travel around the world and back again while the truth is lacing up its boots."

"The father of lies" is indeed an apt and accurate name for Satan. Deception disguised as appealing light is not a bad summary of the demonic job description. This chapter will examine the appeal of the deceptive transaction, the satanic agenda fomenting intentional and subtle resistance to the clear teachings of Jesus, and how I've come to believe that the devil is real.

Bring your own skepticism and disbelief along as we examine these old stories together. Satan goes by many names. It doesn't really matter what you call it, this power of evil. It does matter greatly that any of us ponder thoughtfully the real consequences of such deception, described in a statement about evil penned by theologian and feisty attorney William Stringfellow in his book, *An Ethic for Christians and Other Aliens in a Strange Land* (written in 1964), under a section titled "Demonic Tactics and the Prevalence of Babel": "A rudimentary claim with which the principalities confront and subvert persons is that truth in the sense of eventful and factual matter does not exist. . . . The truth is usurped and displaced by a self-serving version of events or facts, with whatever selectivity, distortion, falsehood, manipulation, exaggeration, evasion, concoction necessary to maintain the image or enhance the survival or multiply the coercive capacities of the principality."[4]

4. Cited in Bill Wylie Kellerman, ed., *A Keeper of the Word:*

"Flood the zone with shit," says political strategist Steve Bannon and his ilk. Pontius Pilate lives. What is truth indeed?

One of the saddest lines in John's Gospel appears early. "He came to what was his own, and his own people did not accept him" (John 1:11). *His own people.* Jesus came into this broken world to heal and unite its residents. There was, is, and will be evil resistance to this radical and holy mission, even within the church—resistance, claims the Nicene Creed, that has been occurring for centuries in realms both "seen and unseen."

*

In the title tale of Karen Russell's excellent collection of stories, *Orange World*, a young woman, Rae, pregnant and worried, strikes a deal with the devil, who roams her neighborhood at night, disguised as a deceptive fox.

> Rae was not raised with religion, so when she sees the blood in the toilet she invents her own prayers. After the results from the third set of tests come back, she starts begging anything that might be listening to save her baby.
>
> And then, lo, something does answer.
>
> *I can help you.* It spoke without speaking, glowing low on the horizon. She had made it over the ledge of 4 a.m. to 5 a.m., what she'd once believed to be a safe hour. The out-of-the-woods hour.

Selected Writings of William Stringfellow (Grand Rapids: Eerdmans, 1994), 215.

What are you?
The voice tipped out of the red light.
That's the wrong question. What would you like me to do?[5]

I used to get not infrequent telephone calls from worried parents, strangers, who wanted me to perform a quick baptism for their new baby—that day, if possible. I would agree to meet with the parents but always asked, "Why do you want this ancient sacrament for your child?" Their answers often ranged between (1) a perceived and holy shield from unexpected calamity or mishap; (2) fire insurance, so to speak, granting a future place in heaven (as opposed to "the bad place"); and (3) belief in baptism as a quasi-magical talisman, an ecclesiastical rabbit's foot, granting lifelong protection from truly evil forces.

Curiously, following the accounts of his baptism in the first three gospels,[6] Jesus is led by the Spirit of God into the wilderness to be tempted by the devil. Look up the three accounts (Matt. 3:13-17; Mark 1:9-11; Luke 3:21-22) and you'll discover that Jesus hardly has time to towel off at the Jordan River before he's ushered into a tense encounter with the demonic. In Mark, the language is especially stark and surprising: "And the Spirit immediately drove him out into the wilderness"

5. Karen Russell, *Orange World and Other Stories* (New York: Vintage Books, 2019), 235.

6. John's Gospel, if you're wondering, assumes Jesus's baptism but does not describe it.

(Mark 1:12). Sheesh. Far from being some magical dousing protecting Jesus from any evil encounter, baptism seems to hasten such a demonic struggle. This is not an easy idea to describe for worried parents seeking sacramental protection for their child. Baptism is a call to confront and resist evil, standing up to Satan and all his empty promises. Read slowly verse three of Martin Luther's famous hymn, "A Mighty Fortress Is Our God," written around 1527:

> Though hordes of devils fill the land
> All threatening to devour us,
> We tremble not, unmoved we stand;
> They cannot overpower us.
> Let this world's tyrant rage;
> In battle we'll engage!
> His might is doomed to fail;
> God's judgment must prevail!
> One little word subdues him.[7]

Jesus cared about poor people, world peace, children, and marginalized folk who felt left out and discarded. But any depiction of the man that fails to mention this core component of his job description is offering less than the full picture: *Jesus came into this world to engage and confront sin and evil, showing those who follow him how to resist temptation authored by the devil.*

The gospel writers waste no time in getting right to the heart of Jesus's purpose. God wants him in the wil-

---

7. *Evangelical Lutheran Worship* (hymn 504).

derness, resisting and talking back to evil. The Lord's Prayer includes the famous petition, "Lead us not into temptation." But the Spirit here oddly "leads" (Matt. 4:1) Jesus posthaste into that very place of tempting, modeling the way of resistance and showing his followers the way to confront and talk back to deception and false promises.

Before examining specific miracles involving Jesus and the demonic, I want to linger a bit here in the desert with this famous encounter, using the version found in Matthew 4:1-11. Three clear temptations raise the curtain on the ministry of Jesus, who'd barely turned thirty, an age when serious themes of deception can lead to ethical consequences that may accompany us for a lifetime. Russian novelist Fyodor Dostoevsky (1821-1881) once made a remarkable claim about this story: "If all the copies of the Bible were destroyed and only this old narrative was left, it would be enough to save us." That's quite a claim. Let's see whether it rings true.

Jesus is fasting for these forty days, a number that might call to mind the forty years of wandering and testing in the wilderness for the Israelites on their way to the promised land. "Remember the long way that the Lord your God has led you these forty years in the wilderness, in order to humble you, testing you to know what was in your heart" (Deut. 8:2). Openly distrust express conversion to the ways of Christ if you're considering signing on with the man. The early church knew the wisdom of lengthy and protracted spiritual formation that modern Christians have largely and regrettably lost, as we claim we're all too busy to devote time to such.

If you're inclined to explore Christianity, here's some advice: locate a congregation that offers spiritual formation opportunities featuring depth and rigor. Jesus offers a sobering warning toward the end of the Sermon on the Mount: "Enter through the narrow gate; for the gate is wide and the road is easy that leads to destruction, and there are many who take it. For the gate is narrow and the road is hard that leads to life, and there are few who find it" (Matt. 7:13-14). An ominous bit of advice offered just before his warning about false spiritual prophets.

Humility and matters of the heart comprise a long-term theological project with no easy shortcuts. Jesus would later pick up on this imagery of the heart in his own ministry—angering religious leadership of his day who were obsessed with outward purity measured by rule adherence—when he said, "For it is from within, from the human heart, that evil intentions come" (Mark 7:21).

Jesus was very concerned about the inner life, the thoughts and hopes shaping our imaginations and waking desires. There's ample darkness in the deep recesses of anyone's heart, including pastors like me. Someone once said, "If we were judged on our inner thoughts alone, we'd all be in jail." True enough.

So, please hear this. Very few people wake up one Tuesday morning and say, "Gee, this seems like a fine day in April to commit adultery or rob my neighborhood bank." Evil, dark deception, instead percolate slowly in the human heart; temptation titillates over steeped time. Each of the seven deadly sins—vainglory (pride), envy, sloth, avarice (greed), wrath, gluttony, and lust—find their origin in the dark corners of the human heart.[8] Jesus was far more interested in the darkness swimming around there than a bunch of outward rules of self-righteousness and hypocrisy that might somehow foster purity with a God waiting to pounce. His attention centered upon *internal life* as much as eternal. It's an undeniable truth that some of the fiercest battles we fight occur when we are completely alone, internally pondering our next steps.

Jesus chose fasting early in his ministry to reveal what was rummaging around in his own human heart, confronting all that might potentially draw him away from God at the very onset of his public ministry. British writer Jim Crace, in his wonderfully imagined novel titled *Quarantine*, retells the story of this lengthy fast. Much of the novel occurs in a cave where Jesus spends hours each day—hungry, alone, and cold. "No one had said how painful it would be, how first, there would be headaches and bad breath, weakness, fainting . . . or how his tongue would soon become stuck to the up-

8. See Rebecca Konyndyk DeYoung, *Glittering Vices: A New Look at the Seven Deadly Sins and Their Remedies* (Grand Rapids: Brazos, 2020). DeYoung's book is the most compelling and accessible treatment of this topic in recent memory. She offers fascinating history and practical disciplines for new and longtime Christians.

per part of his mouth, held in place by gluey strings of hunger, so that he would mutter to himself or say his prayers as if his palate had been cleft at birth; or how his gums would bleed and his teeth become as loose as date stones."[9]

The devil, "the tempter" (Matt. 4:3), arrives while Jesus is facing unimaginable hunger, physical weakness, and perhaps wondering about the nature of his peculiar call. Such a lengthy fast, however, may not necessarily suggest *spiritual* weakness. Fasting and other biblical disciplines have been used for centuries in the church to develop spiritual strength in naming and confronting evil and temptation. "Intermittent fasting" is all the rage these days as a way to lose weight. In the wilderness with Jesus, the focus centers upon the development of spiritual strength. The congregation I served in Virginia offered periodic overnight retreats featuring fasting and silence. The conversations that ensued after we broke the silence were always both revealing and empowering.

It's fair to ask at this point, What does this devil look like here and elsewhere in the Gospels? In the year 1650, Rembrandt, the great Dutch artist, made a pen and brush drawing of this wilderness temptation scene, and the devil is graphically shown as a skeleton with a tail and bat wings. But nowhere in this story is the devil physically described.

In his famous depiction of organized devilry, *The Screwtape Letters*, C. S. Lewis places experienced (and

9. Jim Crace, *Quarantine* (New York: Picador, 1998), 157.

sometimes amusing) demonic advice on the lips of Uncle Screwtape, who sagely counsels his young nephew, Wormwood, in the art of deception. Here's some of the unctuous uncle's advice from early in the book: "The fact that 'devils' are predominately *comic* figures in the modern imagination will help you. If any faint suspicion of your existence begins to rise in his mind, suggest to him a picture of something in red tights, and persuade him that since he cannot believe in that . . . he therefore cannot believe in you."[10]

Nowhere in the Gospels is Satan nearly so obvious. Here in the wilderness, the tempter arrives with three appealing possibilities that actually look quite good—bread for a very hungry man; a circus trick to impress the masses and increase his popularity; power and wealth to possibly expand the reach of his ministry. None of these temptations, at face value, seem demonstrably evil. Satan often offers a subtle and rather enchanting means, cloaked and disguised, to a desired goal.

Lucifer lives—again, "one who bears light."

Note that these three offers all have a single small word in common: the little word "if." There is normally a tease, a taunt, or a transaction associated with the demonic. (Ironically, this is also an accurate depiction of the American political scene with leaders who mock mercilessly and demand unquestioned loyalty in transactional exchange for the acquisition of various desires.) The devil dares Jesus (and us) to eclipse the boundaries

10. C. S. Lewis, *The Screwtape Letters* (New York: Bantam Books, 1982), 19-20.

of healthy personhood and to taste the headiness of the divine. In some ways, the temptations of this story echo the serpent-like lure found in the early pages of the book of Genesis. "You will not die. . . . You will be like God" (Gen. 3:5).

At stake here in the wilderness is the future nature of Jesus's ministry (and ours, if we choose to follow him). Will this life be about sacrifice for others, or glorification of self? About bringing holy attention to the creative wonder of God who made the world and everything in it, or garnering fame and name recognition featuring impressive personal achievement? About sensing truth and grace in a community focused upon love and care for all, or amassing power to bend at least a portion of the world to my personal will and sway? These are questions with answers assuming more intrigue and difficulty than the easy either-or. That is part of the lure and creativity of the demonic: the bad choice often looks enticingly good.

Why *not* turn stones into bread, after all? Good Lord, the man is famished. He'll later famously turn several loaves and a few fish into a meal for thousands of hungry people, right? What's wrong with wiggling his nose and dialing up some doughy Dhebra?

It's the condition posed by the devil. Again, that little word "if" offered as demonic taunt. Prove it, wise guy, if you are indeed the Son of God. Jesus refuses to manipulate his divine connections to demonstrate his merit and worth, even for something as basic as his own urgent and pounding hunger. Instead, he quotes the Bible. Three times he quotes it, all from the book of

Deuteronomy. There he locates his handy road map, his Satan-slapping retort.

Read slowly the scriptural response to his first temptation: "One does not live by bread alone, but by every word that comes from the mouth of God" (Deut. 8:3). Recall the imagery, from chapter 1 of this book, where Ezekiel is told to "eat this scroll that I give you and fill your stomach with it." The food of Jesus that allows him to resist each of the temptations are the stories of power, liberation, love, obedience, and justice that filled his childhood and now fill his fasting imagination and growling stomach to give him courage to resist and shape a life formed and fed by the word of God. Jesus is famished from the lack of earthly food, no doubt, but full of a different sort of food. It is this latter food that wards off the demonic for Jesus, and for any of us. To be steeped in the wonder of God's word, shaped over time by a holy narrative and its incumbent divine direction, is a central message here in the wilderness explaining how Jesus hangs on.

Next is a field trip with Lucifer to the holy city, a place of pilgrimage with a holy edifice very close to Jesus's heart. Drawn to its history and heart as a boy, this is where a twelve-year-old got lost in wonder in the temple, worrying his parents, impressing the elders with his childhood wisdom (Luke 2:41–52), and where he would eventually cleanse the place of religious pretenders in righteous anger (Mark 11:15–19). This is the city he will weep over before his crucifixion (Luke 19:41–44). The city where the Christian church finds its earliest origins (Acts 1:12–14).

The second temptation is again seeded with a devil-ish if-then condition. If you are God's chosen one, do an impressive half gainer with a full twist off the pinnacle of this famous structure. Don't worry; your angels will protect you. It's worth noting here that the devil also quotes the Bible (Ps. 91:11-12), almost waving it around in the face of Jesus like some magic totem in DC's Lafay-ette Square, proving holy credibility. Like some high-wire act between skyscrapers, this acrobatic exploit would surely attract public notice and instant fame. Jesus returns to Deuteronomy. "Again it is written, 'Do not put the Lord your God to the test'" (Deut. 6:16).

I recall an incident that occurred several decades ago at a lake spot—popular with college students on the weekends—near my current residence in upstate South Carolina. It was great fun to walk out on a narrow plat-form and jump to the left into the deep lake pool formed by a small concrete dam. The idea was to swim out to the middle of the slippery dam (slick with algae and a thin sheet of flowing water), carefully arrange your butt in a sitting position, slide sixty feet to the bottom in cut-offs, climb up a steep muddy bank, and gleefully repeat the whole process. It was a bit daring but largely safe and fun, even with a couple beers under your belt, and brought lots of laughter on a hot summer afternoon.

On a break from summer employment at a nearby camp, I stood one weekday afternoon on the platform perched high above the bottom of the dam that contin-ued to angle, unseen, into deep and dark water. A friend and I had the place to ourselves. I'd seen guys forgo the easy jump into the lake pool to the left, instead making the long arcing dive out over the dam all the way to the bottom. I still recall a palpable inner voice saying, "You're young and strong, Frank. It's not that far. You can do this. It'll be impressive, memorable." My friend, Mike, stood behind me on the platform, trying to talk me out of the idea.

Bending my knees and pushing off, I could tell right away what an insanely bad choice this was, feet rolling over the top of my head in middive. I hit the water at such a severe angle, missing the concrete base of the dam by a couple feet, sliding deep along its slippery submerged surface on my back, tumbling around and losing all sense of orientation, finally popping up, needing air. I somehow emerged with only a few scratches and a bruised ego, then swam over to the bank, rested a bit, and considered how utterly stupid and extremely fortunate I'd been. Mike shouted down, a bit irked, asking whether I was okay, and said he'd had visions of running for the EMT squad. Diving accidents leaving people paralyzed still trouble my dreams.

There have been other times I've heard this rather eerie internal voice inviting me to consider something beyond rational or ethical boundaries of common sense. Perhaps you've heard it, too. I'm hesitant to refer to each instance as "the devil," but I have come to believe that Satan indeed whispers to us regularly and enticingly, exploiting our common fascination with power, distinction, notoriety, and fame.

This is the voice Jesus hears on the pinnacle. Jump, you're powerful, you'll be famous. God will protect you. There are few things as sweet as the gift of human freedom, and few things as tragic as the aftermath from abusing this gift. Once we are in the air of a bad choice, God can do little except watch us crash. There is a certain momentum from a realized temptation that is not reversible. Temptations to which we succumb are forgivable, of course, but their consequences are often scarring and may last a lifetime.

Radio personality Garrison Keillor once whimsically said, "If you didn't want to go to Minneapolis, then why'd you get on the train?" There is honesty and truth in this candid question. We do have the wherewithal to resist and say no, refusing to board the train. But the temptation is often so attractively packaged and the voice of invitation so seemingly truthful, packaged as "light," that resistance requires prayerful and serious reflection. If Saint Paul is correct in describing this conflict as a spiritual skirmish "against the cosmic powers of this present darkness" (Eph. 6:12), we'll need more that our own best efforts in the ongoing fight. It's worth pondering this important question: What's regularly shaping my identity over the long haul, providing a daily defense to resist bad choices perhaps authored by the demonic?

Recall the exchange between the sly nocturnal fox and the worried young woman in Karen Russell's short story, "Orange World." She initially wanted to know about the fiendish origin of the compelling voice in the night. Shifting quickly to the transactional, the fox's reply covers quite a few ethical temptations faced by any of us. *That's the wrong question. What would you like me to do?*"

Temptation can be darkly subtle. Many deals exist that we might make with the devil, notoriously adept at exploiting our human need for security and success, both often fueled by our fear of the future. Many false saviors step forth in this life, promising to allay these fears.

For Jesus, it was his familiarity with another more powerful voice—the narrative found in Scripture that radically shaped his confident identity, forming a rather sassy ability to talk back to and defeat evil. Recalling Martin Luther's famous hymn cited earlier, the third stanza (describing this demonic struggle) ends rather ominously: "One little word subdues him." Eat this book, indeed—an enterprise much more involved than just quoting the Bible randomly or waving it around magically in a city square.

The third temptation takes place on a high mountain. Contrast the view from this high peak ("all the kingdoms of the world") with the view from the Mount of Transfiguration, discussed in the previous chapter. One view offers influence, wealth, and godlike power, a tempting invitation that could surely assist the expansion of the fledgling movement Jesus is just starting to lead. The other view (with Moses and Elijah) recalls Jesus's immersion in a very old story and leads to a life of sacrifice and eventually the cross, an odd sort of power indeed. Commenting on this strange sacrificial power, Saint Paul writes, "God chose what is foolish in the world to shame the wise; God chose what is weak in the world to shame the strong" (1 Cor. 1:27). God intentionally chose the foolish and the weak to overcome the world's idea of power. This is not an idea that anyone, even Jesus, can fully embrace on one's own.

Again from Deuteronomy (6:13), Jesus confronts the third temptation with a biblical truth that wealth and power can quickly become idolatrous and take the place of God. Everyone worships something in this life. Everyone has a god. Martin Luther offered a still-accurate definition of a god: "that to which we assign ultimate allegiance." Numerous gods come to mind in the various realms in which any of us daily live.

This third scene raises an important set of questions: Who (or what) am I worshiping with my time, money, and skills? To what do I pledge ultimate allegiance? Satan, the lightbearer, is crafty. Again, temptation does not necessarily look bad. It often masquerades in promised realities that look quite good.

The devil finally leaves Jesus alone, for now. "Suddenly angels came and waited on him" (Matt. 4:11). Forces of light and good are there to assist Jesus (and us, presumably) after this demonic skirmish, but the angels do not (maybe cannot) fight Jesus's battle for him. Another version of this story reports that the devil departs from Jesus "until an opportune time" (Luke 4:13). Temptation, on this side of the grave, is always open-ended and recurring.

Jesus survives this encounter by quoting parts of an old story that fed and nourished him with spiritual food whose power surpassed any temptation thrown his way, enough to send the devil packing. His three recitations from the book of Deuteronomy are all taken from a nearby part of the same book—the great Shema, one of the most famous parts of the Old Testament:

> Hear, O Israel: The Lord is our God, the Lord alone. You shall love the Lord your God with all your heart, and with all your soul, and with all your might. Keep these words that I am commanding you today in your heart. Recite them to your children and talk about them when you are at home and when you are away, when you lie down and when you rise. Bind them as a sign on your hand, fix them as an emblem on your forehead, and write them on the doorposts of your house and on your gates. (Deut. 6:4-9)

Jesus had it in him to call down any number of celestial tricks to defeat evil in the desert so long ago. He chose instead to employ a saving word (available to any of us) that was portable and steeped in the truths of Moses and Elijah. This word was such a large part of Jesus's identity that his life cannot be examined or understood without it.

*

I can think of several dark and eerie places from my childhood that gave me the willies. An old woman, Mrs. Connor, lived alone in the expansive woods that bordered our neighborhood in Chattanooga. Certain she was cooking gingerbread men in a hot oven to lure unsuspecting children to their gruesome deaths, my friends and I would tiptoe up to her porch like moths drawn to the flame. The big dare was to touch her porch railing and run home without turning to stone.

Even as an older teenager, I was consistently unnerved by the feeling of something sinister in the large attic of my grandparents' house in the mountains of North Carolina. It didn't help that my mother claimed to have seen a ghost in that attic. The silky cobwebs, upright files of old letters and military artifacts from the First World War, sheet-covered furniture, and headless mannequins together created a spooky set in my teenage imagination that rivaled any horror movie I'd seen, including *The Exorcist* (1973) or *The Omen* (1976). I never ventured into that attic alone.

I suspect you can name your own places that stirred a variety of childhood phobias. Our middle daughter, Marta, once let loose with a blood-curdling scream from the basement of our home in Virginia. We rushed to investigate and found her huddled in a corner, grabbing us for dear life. "I thought I was home alone," she finally explained, not long after seeing the famous film with the same name. Abandonment to the sinister forces of an often-malevolent world creeps into our imaginations and dreams at an early age.

There was one place, however, where I felt entirely safe and protected—a church building. Holy, set apart, filled with stained-glass light of the saints and tales of good triumphing over evil. Nothing could get me (or anyone) in such a place, sheltered under the protective gaze of God. I figured my early boredom with church in general was a fair tradeoff for the benefits of divine protection that would accompany me through other days of the week for just stepping foot past the holy threshold on Sundays.

*

The Gospel of Mark mentions demons and unclean spirits with some frequency, more than any other gospel. Jesus silences, rebukes, and casts out the demonic in a variety of instances with both children and adults. He speaks with demons, puts them in their place, and defeats them. Not a few commentators attribute these instances to mental illness—especially dissociative identity disorder, once called "multiple personalities"—in a prescientific era, before we understood such things. Highly regarded psychologist Scott Peck (1936–2005), however, once a skeptic of demonic possession, writes of attending an exorcism in one of his books, *People of the Lie*, that left him shaken. Various Christian church expressions (notably the Roman Catholic Church) train specialized exorcists, some part of a team that also includes psychiatric professionals.

Our church secretary, Amy, fielded an urgent phone call one Monday morning from a woman who asked whether our church performed exorcisms. "I can't remember the last one," she deftly replied.

I've never attended an exorcism. Nor have I met anyone who claims to have been healed through one. But I have encountered people who have behaved so deceptively and consistently over time, filled with palpable evil, that I'm not willing to attribute demonic possession to an unusual mental illness. A serial murderer I met during a prison chaplaincy comes to mind—the nicest

person, outwardly, you'd ever want to talk to. I gave
him Holy Communion (at his request) in prison one
Thursday afternoon. He murdered another inmate two
weeks later with a bomb that exploded upon turning on
a radio. I'm convinced, in retrospect, that this man was
seeking some twisted preabsolution (with the body and
blood of Christ) for a crime he'd hatched in his head for
quite some time. I've also known other people so full of
lies, deception, and venom toward others and even an
entire community that I'm left wondering about what
sinister voice they're listening to, wittingly or unwit-
tingly—a voice I've occasionally heard in my own heart
and soul.

I'm aware of the danger here in opening the door to
seeing shades of the demonic everywhere, in any sort
of odd behavior. A Tobias Wolff short story, "Awake"
(first published in the *New Yorker* magazine), describes
this concern. A character in the story, reflecting on the
devil, discovers the existence of "certain priests who cast
out demons as a specialty. That was their job, their mar-
ket niche, waiting around like firemen for the alarm to
go off. Demon in Idaho housewife! Demon in Delaware
bus driver!"[11] All strange behavior cannot be attributed
to the excuse of "the devil made me do it." However, I'm
convinced, for the record, that some strange behavior
can indeed find origin with the satanic.

In Mark's Gospel, just after the temptation encounter with Satan in the wilderness, Jesus calls his first

11. Tobias Wolff, "Awake" *New Yorker*, August 25, 2008, 67.

disciples. They travel together to Capernaum, a seaside village where several events from Jesus's ministry will occur. Here in Capernaum, Jesus will experience his first recorded encounter (Mark 1:21–28) with palpable evil. The setting for this encounter, especially given my childhood understanding of divine protection, is a bit surprising.

Jesus's initial encounter with demonic possession does not occur in some shady, out-of-the-way place like Mount Doom in the region of Mordor, dark clouds and wind whipping across the horizon and all that. No, this initial encounter occurs in a synagogue. There are notable differences in the respective worship spaces, but you might as well call this a church. Christians should linger over this old story. There's a tendency among pastors like me to locate evil somewhere *out there* in a host of bad things, bad people, and compromising situations—in short, with those who are not gathered inside the safe confines of a church building. Organized evil, however, initially raises its ugly head in Mark among those who assemble on the Sabbath to praise God. Ponder that. It's also these same demons who seem to know who Jesus is and what is at stake. The twelve disciples remain unusually obtuse throughout Mark's Gospel and consistently resist where Jesus is leading them. Ponder that also.

The drama of this story is profound. Eerie voices are silenced; a convulsive tongue is healed—the relative weirdness of exorcism. "Could that have really happened?" our modern minds ask. It's worth noting *how* this exorcism occurs. Jesus is not waving a magic wand or wiggling his divine nose. What is Jesus *doing* in that synagogue on that Sabbath day? Only twenty verses into this earliest gospel, Jesus takes on evil in a surprising context. But the demons in this story do not emerge during the church coffee hour or monthly business meeting.

Their chatty interruption occurs as Jesus begins to teach. "Just then" (Mark 1:23), the text reports a loud and rather wild man who chattily accuses Jesus and claims to know his true identity. All of this occurs after his teaching begins, not before.

There is often a tendency in church life to embrace the benign and offer a tame Jesus who never rocks the boat. Schedule an array of outings, athletic teams, worthy fundraisers, and fun social events. Sprinkle a bit of Jesus lite into Sunday morning gatherings. Call that church, the pastor leading a comfortable cruise ship where everyone is welcome and no one is offended.

I caught myself several times as a working pastor asking myself, "What are we doing here? What is our central purpose?"[12] The demons come out among this holy assembly when Jesus starts teaching. Radical teaching (which leads to radical change) will be resisted in church life, even among pastors like me.

Think of the best teachers you had in your past. I suspect they made you think in a way that invited change.

12. See Douglas J. Brouwer, *Chasing after Wind: A Pastor's Life* (Grand Rapids: Eerdmans, 2022). Brouwer candidly reflects back on his pastoral career.

Change is never easy. I had an excellent teacher in high school, Mr. Warner. We called him Joe Baby behind his back, covertly, imagining some secret life for this older single man. He was all business and had a serious gaze that could surely crack granite. You knew why you were there in his class, no guessing about some hidden teacher agenda.

Joe Baby loved Mark Twain. I wrote a reflection paper one Sunday evening (due Monday morning) about the moral quandary of Huck Finn and his relationship with Jim, the runaway slave. I dashed it off in ninety minutes—a passable effort. Mr. Warner returned the paper Tuesday morning. It was covered in ink with a fat red "F" adorning the top of the page with a terse note: "Complete rewrite by tomorrow morning."

Lord, I was pissed, not used to receiving such grades. I wrote with venom and anger and the justice of God on my side.

I waited, smugly. He returned my paper that Friday with *another* bright red "F" and the menacing message: "You're capable of better work than this—start over. Due Monday morning."

Filled with palpable loathing for the little man, I wadded up the paper and threw it in a trash can at home. "Okay, you little jerk. You want to know about moral dilemmas? Who would really care if I let the air out of your tires tonight?" Writing with fire and vengeance, I spent hours on the paper.

He returned it as I left class that Wednesday with a gaze that met mine momentarily before I had to look away. I stuffed the paper in my pack and couldn't look at the thing until that evening at home. "THIS," the man had written, "is what you are capable of." A bold B+ was circled in blue. Mr. Warner was one of the most demanding and difficult teachers I ever had. I learned a lot from him about Twain, other writers, and the writing process. And I'm grateful, fifty years later. But don't get me wrong. I also wanted to wring the man's neck.

Excellent teaching in church life will also be resisted. Jesus (much of the time in the Gospels) offends the status quo and those who try to maintain it. Jesus will bring joy into any life, but if one signs on with the man and he does not occasionally make you mad, pissed even, it's quite possible you've chosen the nonthreatening Jesus adorning Sunday School walls and sanctuary stained glass who's about as risky as milk and cookies, completely harmless.

Demonic forces in this early scene from Mark do everything in their power to distract and divert. Jesus silences these voices of diversion. An exorcism occurs right there in the middle of worship. Perhaps nothing quite as dramatic occurs in church life these days. Our penchant for distraction, however, has never been so tempting, so subtle, and so pervasive.

This was a Sabbath day morning when the spit hit the floor. Jesus flushed out and confronted evil very early in his ministry with a rather surprising mechanism: *his teaching*. If you do not wish to change, no intention of looking at life in a new way, then by all means, stay away from Jesus.

He intends to do business with the darkness in your life and mine. The demons ask, "What have you to with us, Jesus of Nazareth?" (Mark 1:24). The question these days is equally pointed.

What have you to do with me?

*

The story of the Gerasene demoniac (Mark 5:1-20) is among my favorite Bible stories, chiefly because it is so weird. "Consider the lilies," says Jesus, in a teaching about worry and anxiety. I also say to parishioners, "consider the strange." Linger with it. There are so many weird details in this story, waiting to be examined and unlocked with all the mystery and daring similar to entering a distant land complete with fantasy, castles, battles of good versus evil, and locked doors with subtle hints leading to hidden treasure.

I also like the story because it follows directly on the heels of the odd tale of the night sea crossing (examined in chapter 3) with Jesus asleep on the little pillow while his frantic disciples bail water. Are these two stories—a windy nocturnal sea voyage and a possessed man of the tombs—at all related? Be thinking about this question; we'll come back to it.

I'm going to list all the details of the narrative describing this demoniac all at once. Here are several that grab my attention. I'll soon deal with them one at a time:

- Jesus and his disciples arrive at "the other side" of the sea.

CHAPTER 4

- They are met by a naked, howling man who lives in a cemetery.
- He is possessed by a legion of demons who speak and make requests.
- The chatty demons are sent into two thousand swine, drowned in the sea.
- The naked man is healed, clothed, and sent home.
- The pig farmers and other witnesses ask Jesus to leave the neighborhood.

Most of these details are absolutely foreign to our modern sensibilities. Good friends wonder whether I've lost my mind by taking this story seriously.

Richard Beck is a teacher, theologian, and author of the excellent book, *Reviving Old Scratch*, an account of his revisiting (after rejecting) the reality of Satan in the world, particularly through his exposure to stories gathered from inmates through a Bible study he teaches at a maximum-security prison in Texas. Beck writes,

> Five hundred years ago the world was full of supernatural forces, witchcraft, monsters, and ghosts; the world was *enchanted*, rife with "thin places" where the borders between the material and supernatural worlds touched; people could become demon possessed or cursed by witches; the night was full of occult menace and magic; black cats were bad luck. Things are different today. We live in a skeptical age where science and technology define what is "true" and "real." With the advent of electric lighting, the dark forces that haunted the night have been ban-

ished. . . . Modern medicine and psychiatry diagnose schizophrenia rather than demon possession, and we seek out doctors rather than exorcists. [13]

All human beings deal with demons. No one escapes them. We are possessed by *something* that diverts us away from our true self, our true mission—the person God fully intends me to be. With Beck's thoughts in mind, let's examine the rather eerie details hovering around a demon-possessed man, isolated from his community—waiting onshore for disciples who've anxiously crossed to the far side of the sea, and waiting on Jesus who's awakened from his windy nap.

*

If you've decided (at this point in the book) that you're drawn, doubts and all, to a new, in-depth examination of the witness of Jesus in the Gospels, engage in a counting exercise sometime soon in your Bible reading. Count how many times Jesus and his disciples pile into a boat and cross from one side of the Sea of Galilee to the other. These thirteen guys are drawn to the nautical life *a lot*. They sometimes sail against all reason.

The many crossings between two very different sides (Jewish on the west and gentile on the east) of this large body of water—roughly thirteen miles long and eight miles wide—cumulatively begin to suggest more than some manly obsession to row out on the high seas with frequency befitting former fishermen. The church is

13. Beck, *Reviving Old Scratch*, 14.

not yet formed in the Gospels.[14] Certainly shaped by the ministry of John the Baptist, a formal theology of Christian baptism will largely find articulation after Pentecost through the book of Acts and letters of Saint Paul.

Early theologians, however, saw ample teaching potential in the many boat stories circulating orally and their vivid connection to the mission of the early church. Sermons, books, catacomb art, and hymnody all adopted the sailboat as an early symbol of life in the church. Since 1948, the World Council of Churches has used a boat for its main promotional logo. The different cultural and ethnic sides of the Sea of Galilee, separated by and linked through water, became fertile ground for the baptismal imagination of the early church. "As many of you as were baptized into Christ have clothed yourself with Christ. There is no longer Jew or Greek; there is no longer slave or free; there is no longer male and female, for all of you are one in Christ Jesus" (Gal. 3:27–28). The demoniac on the far side of the sea is Greek, or gentile. He is also initially naked, then clothed.

Jesus and his shipmates are headed for "the other side" of the wide water. But there is more going on here than just geography. This sea crossing to an isolated and demon-possessed man is packed with baptismal implications. The boat docks on foreign soil. As soon as Jesus steps out on land, he's "immediately" (Mark 5:2) met by an eerie man of the coastal mist.

14. The word "church" is mentioned only a handful of times in the Four Gospels, all in Matthew's Gospel.

This strange man resides alone in a cemetery. There was some attempt in the budget of the local economy to keep him bound and segregated, an early asylum of sorts, but he broke chains and shackles, no one strong enough to keep him subdued. He howled night and day among the tombs and in the mountains, roaming, bruising himself with stones in repeated incidents of self-harm. The poor man is never named, heightening his isolation.

I was a student chaplain at Central Correctional Institution (built in 1867) on the Congaree River in Columbia, South Carolina, before it was finally torn down. There was a bleak subterranean section of the prison that saw very little light. Segregated there were inmates then known as "the criminally insane," difficult to handle in a residential treatment setting, a danger to themselves and the general inmate population. These men were housed in separate cells and sometimes stripped themselves naked, yelling. I think of a man I would try to talk to some, below ground, in this old archaic unit. His name was Leonard. He spat on my good friend once, right in the face, and howled at the top of his lungs at other times. It was hard to keep returning to a darkness both embodied by the inmate and constructed by the state.

The setting among tombs is one of several unclean boundaries crossed by Jesus in this story. To keep the possessed man segregated there provided an arrangement of odd equilibrium in the local neighborhood. It strikes me that as the story unfolds toward his crucifixion for, in part, crossing one too many boundaries, authorities will also want to keep Jesus in a cemetery and certain tomb sealed by a large stone.

Residing within this tormented man of the tombs, the "legion" (Mark 5:9) of demons is surprisingly chatty. They recognize the authority and identity of Jesus. They fear his power over unseen spirits. They offer alternative ideas. Again, it is worth noting here that demonic spirits seem to know who Jesus is and what he's capable of. This demonic cadre is shrewd, distracting, seemingly clairvoyant, somewhat sycophantic, and capable of taking over and directing certain lives. An important distinction between demonic possession and severe mental illness is that the former state acknowledges, is fearful of, and recoils before the surpassing power and presence of Christ. Note that the question, "What have you to do with me, Jesus, Son of the Most High God?" (5:7), is very similar to the demonic question (1:24) posed earlier by the unclean spirit in the synagogue. The demons, in short, know the jig is up when Jesus arrives.

The drowning of the great herd of pigs (5:11-13) is loaded with baptismal symbolism. Early Christian baptism was preceded by weeks of "scrutinies," rites involving self-searching, repentance, and renunciation of the devil and evil spirits, resembling an exorcism in its breadth and power. In several instances in the New Testament, baptism is considered a death, a drowning, leading to new life in Christ (Rom. 6:3-11; Col. 2:12; 3:3; Gal. 2:19-20). Ancient baptismal fonts were quite deep, often cross-shaped, and included steps leading down one side and up the other, suggesting passage from an old life to the new. Early Christians saw a clear sacramental template in the drowning of unclean swine (sin and evil) in the depths of the sea.

Now described as "clothed and in his right mind" (Mark 5:15), the man's healed state of dress is also filled with baptismal possibility, suggestive of the ritual donning of a new white garment after baptisms that often occurred in the nude in early church history, stripped of all earthly adornment, and timed with the rising sun (Son) at dawn on Easter morning. Remnants of such garmenting can be seen in modern baptisms with child sacramental gowns passed down over decades in many families. The use of these garments in the early church, however, suggested a brand-new life after death to the old way of living. "As many of you as were baptized into Christ have clothed yourselves with Christ" (Gal. 3:27). Old divisions cease. Once haunted and bound in tombs, a new community breathes the love of their liberator.

This troubled man of the tombs is rather desperate to remain with his healer after Jesus boards a boat (Mark 5:18) and prepares to head back to "the other side" (5:21). It seems odd that Jesus, who has already called many to follow wherever he leads, instead sends the man back home to his former friends. But this, too, fits the mission of early baptismal liturgies as converts are commissioned and sent to share the love of Christ who crosses boundaries of exclusion with mercy (5:19) and grace. This healed demoniac reveals the difference between the words "disciple" (student) and "apostle" (one who is sent).

Not everyone is happy with this healed man's good fortune. Miracles often have interesting consequences. The farmers are ticked (and fearful) by the equivalent of this porcine titanic and "beg Jesus to leave their neighborhood" (5:17). Certainly the loss of cash (that's a lot of bacon down the tubes) affects the local economy. But I suspect people, primarily, aren't happy with Jesus because the old arrangement of managed and segregated evil has been upended.

Perhaps you're beginning to notice in your own life that it's sometimes a lot easier living *without* Jesus than with him. That may sound rather nutty for a pastor to say, but it's true. Life's really a lot easier without Jesus. The "narrow gate" (Matt. 7:13–14) leads to life, but such a way is difficult. Without Jesus in your life, it's so very easy to segregate undesirables over in a corner of town. Without Jesus, I never have to be overly concerned with the poor. Without Jesus, I can tip my cap to God rather than follow this nut into dark places on a daily basis. Without Jesus, I can keep all my money for myself rather than wasting it on lost causes. Without Jesus, I can be comfortable with exactly who I am and remaining that way until I die.

Don't be too hard on these townspeople. "Go away, Jesus," they say. I may not say that out loud, but if I'm honest, my behavior resembles theirs in a hundred similar ways. "You are welcome *here* in my life, Jesus. But certainly not over there in the dark places."

*

I hope you've been thinking a bit about the possible connection between this story of an isolated demoniac, segregated and alone in a place of shadowy death, and the story we examined in the previous chapter—the windy night crossing with Jesus asleep on the pillow. The two stories occur back-to-back in Mark's Gospel.

There will always be strong resistance to bringing the love of Christ to places and people whom others have given up on and abandoned. Demonic forces thrive in such instances and their perpetuity. These forces can attempt to (1) divert Jesus himself with temptations of relevancy, fame, and power; (2) invade places of worship (Mark 1:21-28), sites of perceived sanctuary, and distract believers from sound biblical teaching with lots of shiny gimmicks in the name of outreach and worldly success; and (3) invite entire (and fearful) communities to marginalize groups and individuals (Mark 5:1-20) in systemic and planned segregation, perpetuating collective blindness to serious need. Issues of immigration, racism, global poverty, and nationalism come to mind. We all learn to live with a certain number of deaths, shocked by very little.

Political leaders exploit various fears with false promises of national security and financial success, often tapping into our deepest personal prejudices. In an era of diminished confidence in Christianity, pastors (like me, I'll confess) are enticed by schmaltzy shortcuts to promised church growth, which results in generations of biblical illiteracy and spiritual formation often about as deep as a pizza pan in order not to scare anyone off. This mix often creates the potential for a church that mimics American culture instead of daring to shape and confront it.

Fiction writer Flannery O'Connor (1925-1964) once said she wrote stories to reveal an "action of grace in a territory largely held by the devil." She also admitted her stories were usually read "by an audience which puts little stock either in grace or the devil." The power of Satan is often overlooked in its utter mainstream normalcy. Lucifer, the lightbearer, likes it this way, I suspect.

*

One of my favorite novels from the last couple decades is *The Testament of Gideon Mack* (2006) by a Scottish writer, James Robertson. The book received positive attention in the United Kingdom but was largely ignored in the United States. The title character is a rather jaded pastor who no longer believes the claims made in his feeble sermons, or the authority of the Bible upon which much of his work is supposedly based. Pastor Gideon largely finds meaning and purpose in raising money for good causes in his small Scottish town.

One day he goes out for a jog and notices that a neighbor's dog is caught in the current of a swiftly moving stream. Gideon jumps into the water and disappears in a strong cataract, presumed drowned. The narrative takes a strange twist: the agnostic pastor is rescued and clothed by the devil. Gideon spends several days under the river in a dark sort of underworld, engaging Satan in long conversations about demonic purpose and the state of the planet Earth. These chats will become Gideon's testament once he returns to the congregation who thought he was dead. The devil encountered by Gideon is a rather dejected entity: "I used to have a purpose. We both had a purpose, God and me. Now? I just go from one window to another and stare out. Or stare in. Sometimes I do a few conjuring-tricks, push a button here, pull a lever there. But my heart's not in it. Basically, I don't do anything anymore. I despair, if you want the honest truth. I mean, the world doesn't need me. It's going to hell in a handcart, if you'll excuse the cliché, without any assistance from me."[15]

I can certainly sympathize with friends who disbelieve in any metaphysical reality that features a struggle "against the cosmic powers of this present darkness, against the spiritual forces of evil in the heavenly places" (Eph. 6:12). Belief in God alone is a challenge on many days. Factor in God's nemesis, and it all seems too much.

"Holy shit, Frank," I recall a good friend saying. "You invite me to consider these far-fetched stories as the very *Word of God*. And now you want me to wrap my head around an actual evil being engaged in an invisible war with the Big Guy?" Satan's self-description in *The Testament of Gideon Mack* is about as far as many people of my acquaintance are willing to go in terms of demonic influence: "the world doesn't need me. It's going to hell in a handcart . . . without any assistance from me." To believe in the "seen and unseen," as the Nicene Creed puts it, is a difficult concept for many of my friends.

And yet, Americans are drawn to and captivated by movies and books describing supernatural events, ghostly specters, and evil apparitions, something out

15. James Robertson, *The Testament of Gideon Mack* (London: Penguin Books, 2006), 295.

there that is indefinable and unexplainable. There is an odd disconnect between disbelief in God and Satan and the spike in cultural obsession with the unseen. Factor in myriad stories of horrific happenings on the evening news with observers who have no language to describe the horror we're witnessing. "We have an inescapable problem," writes Andrew Delbanco. "We feel something that our culture no longer gives us the vocabulary to express."[16]

I recall a place in Shenandoah National Park in Virginia that my wife and I used to visit with my daughter, Hannah, then a little girl who would fit in a child carrier on my back. We lived near the park for my first call out of seminary, bought an annual pass, and visited often. There was a beautiful and rather isolated place on one of our favorite hikes near Dickey Ridge—deep woods, tall trees.

On every hike into this spot, over several months, Hannah (just learning to talk) would look into the woods and almost whisper these same insistent words: "Et tu, bowie, woods." Cindy and I had no idea what she was saying, but Hannah was riveted upon that same spot many times. She always said those exact words in a hushed tone, locked in on the precise spot in the woods each time we passed it on the trail.

Before the creation of the park, homesteaders lived in sites still visible in places with remnants from stone

16. Andrew Delbanco, *The Death of Satan: How Americans Have Lost the Sense of Evil* (New York: Farrar, Straus & Giroux, 1995), 9.

chimneys. Many families were forced to relocate, leaving behind generational memories, orchards (now overgrown in deep woods) that still bear fruit in season, and dead relatives in cemeteries maintained by the park service.

Years after Hannah repeatedly whispered those odd words, I now think she was saying, "Little boy, in woods." She was perhaps observing a child who used to live in that place, a boy who may have died young. A boy whom Hannah could see, but her parents could not. Children see many things that adults do not. "We move between two darknesses," wrote E. M. Forster. "The two entities who might enlighten us, the baby and the corpse, cannot do so." Children embrace an enchanted realm that soon becomes replaced by scientific explanation.

The Bible assumes that a titanic battle between good and evil is occurring within and beyond human history. "And do not bring us to the time of trial," the Lord's Prayer concludes, taught by Jesus in the Sermon on the Mount, "but rescue us from the evil one" (Matt. 6:13). Jesus engaged an evil presence known by many names. Jesus exorcised people afflicted with evil spirits. Jesus reveals spiritual resources for resistance to and rescue from "the evil one."

Many people suffer from the effects of evil without the assistance of what scholars call a "metanarrative" that makes sense of and gives language to our struggle—an overarching story from which we live our days in a complicated, beautiful, but often dangerous world. The Bible contains such a story where good triumphs over evil in daring and unexpected ways via often odd tales that take awhile to unpack and incorporate into the rhythms of daily life.

"Well and good," you might be saying. But I also detect a question posed so many times by parishioners and others beginning to probe the pages of the Bible, who encounter the marvelous miracle stories of the distant past. We now turn to that question, the focus of the next chapter. "Okay, Frank," you might say, "so Jesus did all this miraculous stuff way back when. What's keeping him from doing it now?"

5

If Jesus Did That Then, Why Not Now?

Jesus began to weep. So the Jews said, "See how he loved him!" But some of them said, "Could not he who opened the eyes of the blind man have kept this man from dying?"

—John 11:35–37

"You're a son of a bitch, you know that? She bought her first new car and you hit her with a drunk driver. Is that supposed to be funny? . . . I think you're just vindictive. . . . Have I displeased you, you feckless thug?"

—*The West Wing* (President Jed Bartlet addressing God in the episode "Two Cathedrals")

People seek out pastors for a variety of reasons: marital troubles, concerns about congregational direction, absolution for sin, guidance for an important decision, and a search for a deeper spiritual life, to mention a few.[1]

In several decades of listening, prayer, and conversation, my vote for one of the top circumstances for contacting someone like me involves meaningless suffering—an automobile accident, an unexpected life-ending disease, a natural disaster—where no one is to blame, no specific sin at the root, no real cause or purpose to examine, a completely pointless event, seemingly empty of meaning.

Christians (and others who are considering the idea of church community) read the ancient biblical miracles and rightly want to know why a miracle man like Jesus does not use his supernatural powers in various modern tragedies like a tragic car accident, the unexpected illness of a child, a storm before widespread suffering and destruction, or with hungry children during

1. Portions of the opening section of this chapter (in slightly different form) first appeared in my essay, "What Kind of God Is This?" *Christian Century*, March 11, 2020, 12–13.

a famine. The question posed by a cluster of citizens in Bethany, Lazarus's hometown (John 11), is as fresh today as then: "If Jesus healed the blind man down the road, what's keeping him from working his magic with this good friend who just died?" Jesus does eventually raise Lazarus from the dead, but the question still stands in all its boldness and honesty in myriad instances of suffering over millennia.

It's easier to handle suffering, I suspect, when there seems to be a *reason* for it—when one can point to something concrete and reflect upon cause and consequence. When no reason is found, even those normally inclined to distance themselves from church often think of God. What sort of God is this? When confronted with meaningless suffering, we often call into question at least one of the points of the omnitriangle (omniscience, omnipotence, omnipresence) normally used to describe God.

"We want to love God with the heart," writes Tom Long, "but we also want to love God with our mind, too. We want to do more than lament and shout and raise the fist; we also want to understand."[2]

One of my favorite letters from Maine that I ever received from my good friend, Andy, was also one of his longest and most pointed. Here's an excerpt:

Dear Frank, . . . Answer these questions. Answer everything in here, dammit. What do you mean by

2. Thomas G. Long, *What Shall We Say? Evil, Suffering, and the Crisis of Faith* (Grand Rapids: Eerdmans, 2011), 130.

God? What is your God? How does your God inter-
act with you? What makes your God important to
you? Define God. Christians see God's work in the
world selectively and see God in the Bible selectively.
What I always think is that God, if anywhere, is everywhere, good and harsh, and if harsh, then we
must make God accountable. If God is revealed in a
sunset, or anywhere in the Bible, then is God revealed
in a bald-headed man I recently met? This man was
born without one single hair. He was a bald-headed
two-year old and 13-year old. That is a tough thing
to do to a little boy. Does that reveal anything to you
about your God, or is your God only in sunsets and
curly-headed babies? God must be more consistent.
If he chooses not to share himself with us, and not
to explain himself, I choose not to respect him. I will
not be rude. God knows where to find me. But if he
wants me for a constant companion, he must stop
being cruel or tell me why.

The letter went on. For fourteen pages it went on and
then concluded, "I will end. I will not sign this letter, and
then perhaps you will not know from whom it came."

Of course, I knew. It was from the same person who
once asked why in the world the pope dressed like an
angel; who promised me that if he ever met God on
the road one fine day, he'd chase the deity down with
a pitchfork; who vowed that if there is a hell and he's a
resident, he sure hopes I know about it.

The biblical response to Andy's questions can seem
rather baffling: God reacts to the suffering of the centu-

ries by, primarily, *sending a sufferer*. God does not pretend to wipe out suffering this side of heaven but instead voluntarily enters it. The miracles described in the Gospels do not begin to touch the vast suffering encountered by Jesus on a daily basis. Was Jesus simply selective in performing miraculous acts? Did he run out of some sort of divinely allotted time he was given to multiply loaves, calm seas, and heal lepers?

Jesus never really attempts to explain the origin of suffering in the Gospels or why it exists. Instead, he walks right at it and the cross: "And what should I say," the church overhears in Lent, "'Father, save me from this hour'? No, it is for this reason that I have come to this hour" (John 12:27).

In John's Gospel, Jesus is quite clear about his destiny and identity. He walks straight at suffering, chooses to carry his own cross (19:17), and says, "whoever serves me must follow me" (19:26)—toward suffering, that is. It's an odd invitation for people who want suffering explained—we who are angry and put out with God for allowing it.

Jesus apparently didn't warm up to this idea all at once. He "offered up prayers and supplications, with loud cries and tears, to the one who was able to save him. . . . Although he was a Son, he learned obedience through what he suffered" (Heb. 5:7-8). This passage is immensely strange but also oddly comforting. Jesus was not preprogrammed. Instead, his wisdom was shaped in the school of suffering.

I resist matriculation in this school. It's a lot easier to talk about why suffering exists than to look suffering straight in the eye and voluntarily enter somebody else's.

I recall a conversation with a thoughtful parishioner who said, "I'm not sure the powerful and important emotion of human compassion is even possible on this earth without some level of suffering among us." I needed that to sink in a bit, but she's right.

Life without suffering is indeed appealing. (I write these words remembering my younger brother, who died recently at age sixty after three agonizing years with brain cancer, glioblastoma, in Washington State.) But a world without compassion is something fundamentally different from life as we now know it. Compassion—*splanchna* in the Greek of Colossians 3:12 and elsewhere, relating to the viscera or guts—cannot exist in our lives without the presence of suffering. There would be no need for compassion in such a world. We would be vastly different people without suffering and the resulting compassion that accompanies it.

I do not believe that God sends suffering as a test or an undercover exercise leading to spiritual maturity. But I do believe God uses our suffering. Entering the darkness of this world shapes and forms us in profound ways we're not able to fully articulate.

Following Jesus, the church walks straight toward the darkness, directly at that which we curse. In learning such lifelong obedience, we discover the one who leads us slowly toward veiled light.

But there are still folk (myself among them) who rail at the divine and wonder why Jesus doesn't use such miraculous power *now* if he did back then. People like

President Bartlet in *The West Wing* after Dolores (his friend and secretary) dies in a random car accident with a drunk driver. Like the worried dad from the introduction to this book who cannot pray for his sick baby even though vast numbers of others are. Like my friend Andy who wanted God "to be more consistent." People, I suspect, who are a lot like you.

*

New Testament theologian Craig Keener pushes back on the assumption that miracles (similar to those found in the Bible) do not happen today. Keener describes his atheism concerning miracles as a young man: "Although some skeptics are open-minded, others place the bar of evidence so high that they will never have to believe. I have friends and relatives who are open-minded, 'agnostic' skeptics, or at least tolerant ones. But there are also dogmatic skeptics and hostile skeptics. When I was an atheist, I was not quite 100 percent dogmatic, but I was hostile; I used to make fun of Christians."[3]

In his book cited above, Keener includes reliable eyewitnesses to modern miracles. He also takes issue with some of the work of various philosophers, particularly Scottish philosopher David Hume (1711–1776), who viewed all reported miracles as violations of the laws of nature. Since natural law cannot be violated, argues Hume, miracles not only don't occur; they can't. Keener

3. Craig S. Keener, *Miracles Today: The Supernatural Work of God in the Modern World* (Grand Rapids: Baker Academic, 2021), 11.

acknowledges that we owe much to modern philosophy, but he rejects Hume's assumptions concerning an inviolable natural law and believes Westerners may have a built-in bias to reject the miraculous, partly due to "false teachings, practices, and miracle claims that pervade some extreme miracle-claiming circles." Evangelist Ernest Angley and his ilk come to mind, as does Steve Martin who brilliantly portrays a crooked faith healer, Jonas Nightengale, in the poignant movie *Leap of Faith* (1992). Keener offers an important insight in reaction to such an understandable skepticism: "Biblically, we are in the era of the foretaste of the kingdom, the time between Jesus's first and second coming—the era of Pentecost. . . . Some Western Christians recognize the Spirit only when God works within accepted structures. Thus they readily welcome some gifts that fit within those structures (especially teaching) while explaining away, and hence rarely experiencing, others. Still, a foretaste differs from the consummation. Miracles foreshadow the world made new, but they do not eliminate the problem of suffering."[4]

Later in the book, Keener admits that those who work in certain fields often see more death than miracles. "I cannot blame many Christians who work in such settings if they develop a certain cynicism towards miracles after witnessing so much suffering. What we call miracles are still the exception rather than the rule."[5]

4. Keener, *Miracles Today*, 15.
5. Keener, *Miracles Today*, 221.

Keener is a compelling teacher and theologian. I agree that rampant and well-documented suffering in the world calls into question the existence of the miraculous. This was certainly the case with my friend, Andy, and with other friends. But it may be worth noting that suffering is not the only reality that may dampen anyone's embrace of biblical miracles. Lurking in the shadows of belief is the reality that some may question your sanity upon taking miracle stories seriously.

I've recently discovered the Irish writer William Trevor (1928–2016), considered at one time by the *New Yorker* to be "the greatest living writer of short stories in the English language." In one of Trevor's fictional stories, "Lost Ground," a fifteen-year-old named Milton Leeson experiences, on successive days, a visitation from a mysterious woman, dressed in black, in his father's orchard in September of 1989. During the second visitation, the woman calls down to Milton from the upper orchard by the gate:

> He could hear her perfectly, although her voice was no more than a whisper.
>
> "I am St Rosa," the woman said.
>
> She walked down the slope toward him, and he saw that she was dressed in the same clothes. She came close to him and placed her lips on his.
>
> "That is holy," she whispered.
>
> She moved away. She turned to face him again before she left the orchard, pausing by the gate to the lane.

"Don't be afraid," she said, "when the moment comes. There is too much fear."

Milton had the distinct impression that the woman wasn't alive.[6]

Milton has no idea what Saint Rosa means by "the moment" or by any fear that might follow from it.[7] The boy consults his pastor who tells him to keep quiet about the visitation. He then visits the local priest who Milton believes may be more familiar with holy kisses and such strange saints. Father Mulhall is angered by Milton's claims and wonders why a saint of his church should appear to a Protestant boy in a neighborhood filled with Catholics.

Milton decides he has to tell people about Saint Rosa's visitations. Despite his parents' objections, Milton travels to nearby villages and preaches on street corners about what he's seen. "He practiced preaching, all the time seeing the woman in the orchard instead of the sallow features of Jesus or a cantankerous-looking God, white-haired and bearded, frowning through the clouds."[8] The boy is subsequently chained in the yard or locked in his bedroom, his parents full of shame and embarrassment by their son's behavior. A psychiatrist

6. William Trevor, "Lost Ground," in *Selected Stories* (New York: Penguin Books, 2009), 110.

7. Born in Peru, Saint Rosa (1586–1617) was the first canonized saint in the Americas. Known for her care of the poor in Lima, she is the patron saint of gardening and blooms, perhaps explaining Trevor's choice in the story to place her in an orchard.

8. Trevor, "Lost Ground," 126.

concludes the boy has gone mad. Milton eventually dies violently, "shot by intruders when he was alone in the house."

As a parish pastor, I stopped counting how many people came to me, almost whispering, with stories that began with the words, "You're not going to believe this." It's not easy to share an experience that's a bit strange and out of the ordinary. It's often easier to just keep quiet.

In her book, *When God Is Silent*, Barbara Brown Taylor asks, "Whatever happened to the talkative God of the Bible? What wouldn't we give for one comforting word in the garden in the cool of the evening, or a commandment so audible it made people cover their heads? . . . For reasons beyond our understanding, the sovereign God is not so talkative anymore."[9] An undeniably true statement. But perhaps the normally loquacious God of the Bible has gone silent in our era not to confound us but rather to protect us from mockery and suspicion like that experienced by young Milton and many others.

*

Let's return to the question that frames this chapter. If Jesus did all that back then, why not now? It's an important question. And regardless of the responses I've attempted in this short chapter, my most honest answer is that I do not know. My frustration with God in this regard sometimes echoes my friend, Andy, who wanted a bit of consistency from the divine.

9. Barbara Brown Taylor, *When God Is Silent* (Boston: Cowley, 1998), 24, 26.

Why there, and not here? Why then, and not now? In a powerful National Geographic documentary, *The Cave* (2019), an extraordinary medical staff cares for victims of war, many of whom are children, in Syria outside of Damascus. The challenges are immense with lack of supplies and staff shortages in a makeshift hospital, partially underground, amid rubble and carnage. One courageous doctor, Dr. Amani Ballour, a young woman in her thirties, asks, "Is God really watching?" The viewer is invited to wonder along with this doctor whether God sees these atrocities and, if so, what the lack of specific divine intervention says about the Creator.

Some people (Thomas Jefferson among them) solve this thorny dilemma of God's seeming absence by resorting to Deism, a system of thought with a God who created the world and its intricacies long ago but who then stepped away with no daily interaction among its inhabitants. This, however, is not the stance of the Bible, which assumes close communion with God via the gifts of the Holy Trinity, including a Spirit who "helps us in our weakness" and "intercedes with sighs too deep for words" (Rom. 8:26).

For several years, I've been intrigued by an old story from the book of Daniel (10:1–21). The setting occurs in Babylon in the third year of King Cyrus (536 BCE) during the long exile experienced by Daniel's people after the fall of Jerusalem. Exile and exodus are two primary historical events in the Old Testament whose recurring themes pepper a large chunk of the Bible. Both events are attributable to divine intervention and purposeful intent. The exodus describes liberation of Israel from an Egyptian captivity realized through no fault of their own. The Babylonian exile occurred after repeated (and ignored) warnings from the prophets to repent and change. Understanding the differences and similarities between these two events will greatly assist your reading of the Old Testament and the incarnation of Christ in the Gospels.

The book of Daniel is filled with fantastic stories about exiles trying to keep the faith in a foreign land— surviving the blazing heat of a fiery furnace (3:19-30) after disobeying the king's decree; prophecies against the ruling elite via mysterious handwriting on a banquet room wall (5:1-30); and taming lions after being cast into a pit for refusing to pray to anyone but God (6:1-28). In some ways, life as an American Christian in the twenty-first century is an exercise in trying to keep the faith in a foreign land, with invitations to bow and pledge allegiance to a variety of competing gods.

Chapter 10 finds Daniel in prayer. One of the reasons I'm drawn to this story is that Daniel is notably *unsuccessful* in prayer. He's struggling with a problem and prays and fasts for many days (10:2-3), weeks, receiving no answer or direction—nothing. This story is perhaps emblematic of anyone's prayer life. There are times when it just seems that no one is listening and we're praying into some thick ether that cannot be penetrated.

After weeks of prayer, Daniel eventually receives a visit and a physical touch (10:10) from an unnamed angel. (Some commentators believe this is Gabriel who later appears to Zechariah and Mary in Luke 1, but there is no evidence for this association in these verses from Daniel). And here the story takes an even more unusual metaphysical turn.

The angel acknowledges Daniel's frustration in prayer over the last weeks and also reports that his prayers have gotten through. "Do not fear, Daniel, for from the first day that you set your mind to gain understanding and to humble yourself before your God, your words have been heard, and I have come because of your words" (10:12). The angel's words here are surely balm to people like me who sometimes wonder whether daily prayer is simply talking to myself. God hears "from the first day." God's response, however, can feel like a lengthy delay.

The explanation for divine delay in answering prayer in this ancient Bible story may conjure in your imagination some titanic wrestling match between the gods in the latest Marvel movie. The apologetic angel who visits Daniel has been delayed due to an epic tussle with a Persian prince in the expansive airspace of that region that lasted three full weeks, the amount of time that Daniel has been asking for help. The angel was able to break away to visit Daniel, our exiled hero, only because his winged rescuer, Michael—in an ancient tag team that surely foreshadowed the birth of the World Wrestling Federation—"came to help me, and I left [Michael] there" (10:13). Michael puts a headlock on the Persian whippersnapper, creating an opportunity for the unnamed angel to break away to Babylon, prayer answered. Got all that?

I love these rather weird details and want to remind you of my earlier advice to consider the strange in these stories. (This book's final chapter will explore this idea in greater detail.) Don't rush past the bizarre in the Bible. After sifting through the many odd twists and turns in this angelic visitation, here's the main message: In language straight from the Nicene Creed, *there are "unseen" forces in conflict with each other that even God cannot unravel with the wave of a hand, sometimes preventing a clear answer to our prayers*. Daniel kept at it for twenty-one days. I've known people who prayed for twenty-one years about a specific problem before clarity emerged. This does not mean that God is not listening. It may mean (in some instances) that the consequences of human freedom are not easy to unravel, even for God. These thoughts do not explain all facets of our original question in this chapter. If Jesus did that then, why not now? But Daniel's prayer life does reveal that divine (even miraculous) response may be more complicated than we know.

6

Virginal Laptop

We've covered a lot of ground in the last few chapters of this book—discovering several general maxims to apply to the various miracles of Jesus, examining specific miracle genres that Jesus experienced both in nature and with the demonic, and pondering divine consistency concerning miraculous stories and events.

Before a final concluding chapter that further invites folk like you to embrace what theologian Karl Barth (1886–1968) once called "the strange new world within the Bible," I'd like to offer a short story about a pastor who has an unusual and whimsical encounter with the Virgin Mary. Part of my intent is that we need a bit of a break, an interlude. But this fictional tale mainly serves as a transition to the book's conclusion, where I'll make a case that faithful scriptural interpretation involves playing with the details of ancient Bible narratives, turning the stories over like a fine and precious stone, its many jeweled facets exposed to divine light attempting to shine forth grace and truth in our world, even now.

Vince mouse-clicks the small white X framed within foreboding red in the upper right corner of the "Wireless Networks Available" pop-up reminder appearing on his computer screen. Ever obedient to thousands of sanctimonious index finger taps, the seventeen-year-old Gateway hums to life each morning as if right out of the box. Somewhat resembling the familiar Amazon logo, a satisfied smile forms alongside Pastor Chary's deep dimples.

"Smug" is not quite the right word to describe his daily morning access to a digital world of keyboard and pixel, as he lacks the lurking dangers of cyberspace. "Wary" surfaces in the seasoned pastor's mind upon returning to his sermon draft, a reflection for the coming Sunday based upon respective domestic structures built upon rock and sand.

Vince Chary has been a pastor long enough, twenty-seven years this fall, that he trusts few things out of sight and touch (parishioner financial pledges come to mind), but especially something as darkly wispy as the Web and its endless privacy-invading tentacles. He sometimes considers how this wariness may be affecting his prayer life with an unseen God.

"Wise words from the master carpenter," Vince reminded his wife, Molly, over fresh peaches and Cheerios. "But Lord Jehovah in heaven, any fifth grader can detect such foundational folly given future forecasts. Look around you, people. Check the weather."

Molly rolled her eyes. She loved the man, but his obsession with alliteration and internal rhyme scheme, effective on Sundays in the pulpit, wore thin around the parsonage, especially for an English teacher.

In his ninth year at New Mount Zion Lutheran, Vince, with prayerful intention, never ran the first virus scan on his laptop or considered, even for an instant, installing the complimentary version of the popular Russian net-nanny, hastily removed (with no little effort) by his clergy colleagues, "suddenly suspicious of the source of such products" since the recent election interference hit the headlines.

"Kluszewski, I think it's called," Vince reported between bites of blueberry bagel.

"No, wrong. That's the baseball player's name," said Molly, who grew up in Cincinnati. "Big Klu, huge fan favorite, played first base. Got his autograph when I was fourteen after he returned to the Reds as hitting coach under Sparky. Loved the man."

"Whatever. Kasplashsky, maybe. Something like that. The whole 'free firewall' pitch really was set up for suckers, don't you think?"

"Vince, it's not like you never visit the internet. You send email to parishioners on our desktop computer. You glance at the swimsuit issue. I saw the history."

The pastor reddened. Vince was surprised and touched that his wife could still embarrass him after a quarter century of marriage.

"Well, the laptop is special. It's my personal writing and all. And I don't want anyone spying. You *have* taped over the camera portal on your own school laptop, haven't you? Even Mark Zuckerberg does that."

"No, I haven't, Vince. Don't you think you're going a bit overboard with all this? I FaceTime."

"Sounds rather racy, doesn't it? Look, I heard last week that Kevin Larson over at Third Pres had all his sermons held hostage by some hacker in Madagascar. Poor guy had to pay three hundred dollars to get them all unlocked. Had no other choice."

"Should have updated his Ransomware protection."

"And that's my point exactly, Molly. When does it all end? All these digital prophylactics? An entire industry incessantly designing the latest protection! You must admit that my trusty Gateway is in excellent shape, internet-free all these years, compared to other laptops half its age. I'd rather have one device that I know is completely safe, utterly virginal. No frills, just word processing. What's the harm in that?"

*

Vince's Friday agenda, barring a parish emergency, was always the same.

Over another bowl of Cheerios and peaches—alarmingly for the pastor, Molly had switched to Grape Nuts and blueberries with a dollop of yogurt—Vince reported the events of the coming day, which his wife already knew by heart.

"First, prayer time. Then, several hours writing the sermon on the Gospel of Matthew's meteorological madness. Then, mowing the lawn followed by trimming and, of course, blowing off the sidewalk and driveway with my new Lowe's lawn lackey. Then, a short bicycle ride and quick shower. Then, an afternoon gin and tonic. Then, languorous lovemaking as a sunset précis to an unforgettable evening feast. Which of those menu items makes your heart flutter the most, my dear?"

"The surface-blowing," Molly replied, between bites.

In his devotional time after breakfast, Vince gave thanks for such a witty wife whose summer break would allow her to keep a morning hair appointment at Kat's Kuts and Kurls. "An unfortunate acronym," he thought, "especially for South Carolina, despite the clever alliteration."

Vince pressed the small circular button on the Gateway, waited for the faithful machine to boot up, and clicked out of the annoying pop-up.

"Rock, sand, floods," the pastor said, almost muttering. "Such pedestrian words—forgive me, Jesus."

Vince smiled as he typed. "Let's use Granite Gneiss. Quintessential Quicksand. Marauding Monsoons. Yes, yes!"

Molly peeked into her husband's study. "Everything okay in here? You sounded on the verge of grateful glossolalia."

"Yes, fine. Smartass."

"I'm off to Kat's. Try to behave yourself."

"Always." Vince blew his wife a kiss and returned to the keyboard.

While writing a sermon, the pastor always spoke aloud—numerous times, with various tonal emphases and inflections—the words of the gospel lesson used as the basis for preaching. It helped Vince get in touch with how the Lord's voice might have sounded to the first disciples and other prospective followers.

"Everyone, then, who hears these words of mine and acts on them will be like a wise man who built his house on rock."

After the seventh reading, testing certain words with various volume tweaks, Vince spoke directly into the computer screen.

"'Everyone, then, who hears.' *Everyone who hears.* Yes, that's the challenge of it, dullards of God. We may listen to the words of Jesus, but do we really hear them? Truly digest their meaning? Remove the earplugs, pugilists of pusillanimity!"

Vince thought he might have to offer a confession to Molly that he had to look up the last word. "Okay, so the image of a cowardly boxer might be stretching a description, however arresting, of the lax faith posture of a parishioner willfully disregarding the word of God."

Intuiting his spouse's objections (an English teacher, after all), the pastor grinned at the keyboard with a raised eyebrow and nonetheless decided to leave the tricky turn of phrase in the final draft.

Later that morning, after rehearsing the sermon several times, Vince began the series of clicks that would turn off his trusty laptop. As always, he planned to read over the sermon one final time on Saturday morning before printing a copy for the pulpit.

A breath before the last click leading to shutdown, the pastor heard a female voice. He first thought the voice was Molly's, as she returned for lunch. She enjoyed fooling with him these summer Fridays near noon in the carpeted hallway.

"Here am I, the servant of the Lord," the voice said.

"It's a little early for that, baby," Vince said with his best Austin Powers accent. "The International Man of Mystery hears the lawn calling first."

"Let it be with me according to thy word."

"I like the sound of that, you randy thing, but do *behave*, my love." Vince thought his impression of Mike Myers was not half bad.

The pastor performed the final mouse-click and peeked through the cracked office door into the hallway. He walked into the kitchen and looked out the window above the sink.

"That Molly," he said. "The clever lass."

Vince finally concluded—after a thorough search, walking outside into the driveway for the day's mail—that his wife had yet to arrive home from her hair appointment.

*

On Christmas morning when Vince was a little boy, he'd run downstairs, open his gifts, deposit the wrapping paper in a garbage bag, and line up the new treasures under his bed, from smallest to largest. He liked knowing where things were.

"You'd save time," he used to tell Molly and his two daughters, both now living in New York City after a childhood in South Carolina, "if you put your keys in the same place each time you walked in the back door. Notice this convenient row of hooks beside the refrig that I installed after we paid the Honda dealership five hundred dollars for your mom's replacement fob that finally showed up three springs later under a row of tomatoes out back. Consider the key hooks, as you might the lilies of the field. That way, we wouldn't have to turn the house upside down each time you lost them. Have you ever thought about how much time you'd save in a year, adding up all the minutes you spend searching for the slippery?"

None of the three females ever answered this question, repeated at regular intervals throughout the year but especially during Lent.

The afternoon that he heard the voice, Vince mixed a gin and tonic for himself and handed Molly her favorite cocktail, something called a Revolver—Bulleit bourbon, Kahlúa, and orange bitters, garnished with a fresh twist of orange.

The pastor measured each ingredient with exact precision, careful not to spill a drop. After two of these, Molly became a different person entirely—perhaps a temptress in a Russian spy novel—far removed from the sensible demeanor of an English teacher married to a respected clergyman. Vince handed her the first round and asked her opinion about the voice, reserving round two for endeavors that usually unfolded after sundown.

"No, it wasn't me," she said. "Promise. Sounds like something I might do, yes. But, as you know, I've been gone for most of the day. Now if we had Alexa, the handy home assistant my girlfriends swear by, we could contact Amazon and maybe find some explanation. But good God, Vince, you look like a deer in the headlights. I've never seen you this rattled since Bonnie ate most of your sermon manuscript early that Sunday morning before church during a thunderstorm, way before you had any backup digital capability. I thought you'd never forgive that dog. I have to admit I loved how you had to wing it later that morning in worship. It's rather seductive when you're out of control just a bit."

Vince looked at Molly's drink glass. It was almost empty. "A little fast out of the gate," he thought.

"This is crazy, you'll undoubtedly agree," he told his wife. "But at one point it sounded like the woman's voice was coming from my laptop. But that's impossible. You know the Gateway is internet-free."

"No, I didn't know that, Vince. Did you mention that at some point?"

Vince again looked at Molly's glass. She'd drained it.

"It's one thing I've always loved about my wife. Her tact. Her patient understanding. Her witty sassiness."

"That's three things."

Vince laughed. "What the hell," he thought to himself, reaching for Molly's empty glass.

"Now this is the really weird thing," Vince said, reaching into the liquor cabinet for the Revolver ingredients.

"Oooh, goody. More near-ineffable and certifiably insane clutter from the clergy cranium."

"Nice alliteration, Teach."

"Thank you, Reverend. I learned from the master. Does this revelation require a double?"

Vince decided he liked this summer vacation version of his wife. "Let's start with one and a half and see if you're speaking in tongues a half hour from now. I'm serious, now please pay attention."

He handed Molly her glass, returned to the rocker, and continued. "I wrote down the woman's two statements word for word. For evidence, I guess."

Vince held up an index card and read aloud. He paused for a moment and let the words settle into a gathering silence, punctuated by Molly's raised eyebrows and a sideways glance to the front door.

"They're from the Bible, you know," the pastor said.

Molly laughed. "The King James Version, I hope."

"Look, I'm cutting you off. Please be serious. I heard a woman's voice come from my virginal laptop and the words were those of the Virgin Mary, resolved to do God's will even though she sounded frightened and confused. Do you believe me?"

"I believe you've been working very hard lately, Vince. And I believe you know the Bible as well as any pastor of my acquaintance. The words were probably swimming around in your imagination as you were writing your sermon."

"But I'm not preaching on that text this Sunday! We're months away from Advent. You know that. And I heard her voice. A real voice."

"I believe you heard something, dear. Didn't your laptop come with some five-minute instructional video you could listen to without an internet hookup? Some Australian woman's voice?"

"Yes. I mean, no! I disabled the damn droning on day one. And why would such a didactic droll be dipping into the Bible?"

Molly rolled her eyes and tossed her empty glass toward the fireplace.

"You missed," Vince said.

"No, I didn't miss. I married the most lovable and messed-up man of any girl's wildest dreams. Isn't summer vacation with an empty nest beyond grand? Now toss back that G and T, join me over here on the couch, and let's see what happens with some afternoon delight and a gal who gave up her virginity a long time ago."

*

Friday mornings at the laptop continued with broadening revelation that summer for Vince Chary. He began to wonder—privately, with no further conversation about these odd encounters with his wife, who'd threatened to call his doctor—whether his Gateway was a bit more than just a brand name.

"Some sort of time-travel portal like that TV show Molly likes where the British lass scoots through the stones for a saucy *sexcapade* with that Scottish lad," Vince thought, smiling at the quintuple cascade of consonants.

On the fourth consecutive Friday morning after her initial revealing and following the previous week's short chat about losing her prescient twelve-year-old son "for three horrid days of worry that time in Jerusalem," the

Virgin Mary—actually no longer a virgin according to most Protestants—asked Vince a question.

"Can I give you a bit of advice?" This was just like Mary, Vince thought: never barging in, always a polite request.

"Please, of course," said the pastor, who'd been working that morning on a sermon about the prodigal son, the lectionary text assigned for the middle of the Pentecost season.

"People hear all about the sordid stench hatched by the younger son," Mary began. "Eusebius, that history hack, who, as you know, toiled three hundred years after my little family ceased to be, was obsessed with that poor boy's failings. I'd focus on the elder brother. That sanctimonious shit gets off the hook too easily if you ask me."

Vince was initially shocked that a woman so biblically pure could use such a word. He was relieved that Mary's disembodied voice could not detect the pastor's facial reaction through a computer screen. On second thought, given the paranormal intersections from the last few Fridays, he double-checked the laptop's mini-camera, carefully covered with tape when the computer was removed from the box fourteen years ago despite the 0 percent chance of the device ever going online.

"Adhesives can break down," the pastor quickly thought to himself. "Like people," the thought continued, unbidden.

"Yes, he does indeed," Vince said, recovering. "The guy reminds me of my own elder brother. I still have time before Sunday for a few revisions. Thanks for the idea."

"Don't mention it," said Mary. "I think that son of mine based this clever tale on fresh interactions with his own brothers. You'll recall those jealous boys thought Jesus went a little crazy there early in his ministry and tried to restrain him. Your Gospel of Mark, chapter 3, yes? Maybe that older brother in the story, the haughty hell-avoider with cow poop on his cardigans, is a composite character based upon the jaded and rather jingoistic gyrations of Jesus's genealogy. I know that last word is debatable, given his daddy and all, but I love alliteration."

Vince couldn't believe his ears. He wondered about the ethics of pirating such a clever phrase for his sermon. The rave reactions from parishioners after worship at the door of New Mount Zion Lutheran the following Sunday convinced the pastor that he'd made the right call in borrowing words he was certain no one had ever heard before, virginal in more ways than one.

*

As the Friday morning Gateway chats came and went like clockwork that strange summer, Vince realized that his preaching had improved.

"You've preached some humdingers lately, my dear," Molly said late one Monday afternoon with a Revolver in her right hand. She slowly swirled the beverage in a counterclockwise motion, sniffing the pungent aroma of the interacting ingredients. "I learned a lot yesterday about the Virgin I'd never heard before."

Lutherans rarely celebrated the festival of "Mary, Mother of our Lord," honored each August 15 on most church year calendars since the sixth century. During the summer of the laptop visitations, the fifteenth fell on a Sunday, so Vince thought, "Why not? Might get these staid Protestants to realize that a lot of church history precedes the bombastic booming broadsides of Brother Martin."

"I've also noticed you seem a lot more relaxed these days," Molly continued. "Is it just the slower summer pace at church, or is something else going on?"

Vince looked at his beautiful wife and knew the moment called for some sort of explanation in his changed clerical tenor. He thought about telling Molly but knew the full truth would only alarm her unnecessarily.

"I think it's my return to an early morning workout schedule," he said, which was indeed partly accurate. Vince had let that part of his life go in recent years due to the time crunch of a frantic pastoral schedule.

"Well, other people are noticing, too," Molly said, winking. She placed her glass on the coffee table, rose from the recliner, and said, "Don't move. I have to pee."

While Molly was out of the room, Vince thought of the latest virginal interaction from last Friday morning. It was easy to get Mary to talk about the Bible text assigned for her special feast day.

"I had other plans, of course," she told Vince. "And I'm sure you can imagine me trying to explain the pregnancy to my parents."

"Not to mention your husband," Vince said. "I notice he never once speaks in any of the stories that became the early church's Gospels. But I'm sure Joseph had a few private opinions about how in the world his beloved bounced around your bustling burg with a bun in the basket, so to speak. I can understand why you wanted to hightail into the hill country there in your first trimester and spend several months with your cousin, Elizabeth."

"I learned a lot about my penchant for control and *how to let go,* as your latter-day therapists put it. I've gathered over these Fridays that you're also a pretty tightly wound—and perhaps wounded—cleric, Vince. May I offer a bit more preaching advice?"

Mary paused, thoughtfully. "I wonder whether your parishioners might benefit if you occasionally let your homiletical hair down, so to speak—a little less guarded, emotionally, in the pulpit."

"Molly tells me the same thing all the time. I'm working on that. Look, I know our time is about up. It won't shock you to discover that I've clocked each of our visitations, and we're now at the eleven-minute mark of the quarter-hour Gateway allotment that always ends at noon. Perhaps recalling the commencement of your son's crucifixion, yes? But speaking of letting go, are you aware of the 1928 painting by Max Ernst, a German artist, with the curious title, *The Blessed Virgin Chastising the Infant Jesus before Three Witnesses*"?

"Oh, yes, the controversial canvas where I'm spanking the little Lord Jesus's belligerent bare bottom? I did absolutely lose it with the boy on occasion. What mom doesn't? Max, however, God love him, takes a bit of artistic license with scriptural evidence. I never owned a red form-fitting dress, for example. And that intact halo as I swat my son's keester is just the sort of thing I tried to distance myself from while struggling with all the challenges of motherhood. You can probably imagine that it wasn't easy serving as the Mom of God."

"No, good Lord," said the pastor.

"Yes, very good," Mary said. "Most of the time."

"I'm planning to use the painting in my sermon this Sunday, your feast day, incorporating our new audio-visual system with stunning synchronous and symphonic sanctuary sensibilities. Just want to let people know you were a real live person with human foibles and emotions."

"And that's just the sort of thing I hope parishioners like yours can discover about their pastor over time. I suspect clergy are placed on a pedestal way too often when they're really struggling with rather pedestrian peccadilloes just like people in the pew."

As if they'd been playing a spirited game of Scrabble, Mary also said, "Very nice six-S word play there a moment ago. Makes my four-P effort look rather paltry."

Vince laughed. "Well, you did work in two others a few words back in the same sentence. I say we tied on that one."

*

After Vince went to bed on the Thursday night before Labor Day, near the end of Molly's summer vacation, she snuck into his study, unboxed a new Dell laptop she'd purchased online at Best Buy, ran through the tutorial, installed the latest virus protection, and connected the shining machine to their local internet provider.

At five thirty the next morning, after their twelfth lap around the lighted walking track at the town park, Molly handed the ancient Gateway to her exercise companion and English colleague, Terry Benson.

"May she rest in peace," Molly told Terry, who departed shortly after breakfast for a long weekend with her husband in Myrtle Beach. On the way, the Bensons planned to drop off several items taking up space in their garage at the Goodwill store in West Columbia.

"I'm sure the clerk at Goodwill," Terry said, "will be ecstatic to receive this."

Vince had to make a hospital call that Friday morning. Lowell Herlong was facing triple-bypass surgery at nine. Vince was home an hour later, planning to return to the hospital that afternoon to check on Lowell.

He called out from the study as if wounded by a gunshot.

"You what?" said the pastor, disbelieving, after his wife explained. Molly was reading the newspaper with coffee in her recliner, looking pleased with herself.

Vince reentered the study, momentarily doubting the swap, then returned to the den. He slowly moved his head from side to side, eyes closed, arms crossed.

"I really thought you'd like it. You said in a sermon recently that you were trying to be more open to surprises and spontaneity. Well, here's a little surprise."

"It's a big surprise, Molly. You know that what I suggest in a sermon and how I really choose to live are sometimes not the same realities."

"Did you actually hear what you just said, Vince?"

"Can you call Terry? Can you intercept the Gateway?"

Molly called her friend. "They're east of Florence, an hour from the beach," she reported back. "Terry dropped off 'your precious' when the store opened at eight. And yes, I called Goodwill. It was out the door by nine."

"I'll bet it was. Molly, I cannot believe you gave away my precious virginal laptop for free."

"Good God, Vince. That sounded like some hackneyed line out of the adolescent romantic chick lit some of my students read. I don't care what you say about the internet and its dangers. This is all about trust, which is a rather weird topic for a pastor to have trouble with, if you think about it."

Vince left the den in silence, retreated to his study, and closed the door, how he usually handled disagreements with his wife. He planned on nursing his disappointment at least through the weekend, a convenient smoke screen (he'd later confess to Molly) concerning the truth she just dared to speak out loud.

He looked at the glowing screen of the new laptop and thought of Mary. Her last bit of advice about letting go of being in control all the time tumbled into the pastor's mind. It was only 10:47 a.m., well before the usual visitation.

The pastor was still staring at the screen ten minutes later when he received a text message from Wilma Herlong saying that Lowell's surgery was going well. It was time to start writing his sermon.

Vince's eyes and fingers raced over the familiar keyboard. Even though he used only two middle fingers to type, the wider set of keys plugged into a side port gave him more room (and, he thought, enhanced creativity) than the cramped, compacted laptop letters of any Dell, Apple, or Gateway that Vince had ever encountered. He once made the mistake of commenting to Maude Henry, a dwarf, one of his favorite parishioners, that "the keyboard of a normal laptop must only fit the fingers of your average Munchkin."

Molly had been kind enough to sense, lovingly, that a different keyboard coupled with a strange and new laptop might completely overwhelm her husband. Thank God, Vince thought, that her inclinations of goodwill did not include the digital harnessing of his two birdie fingers, both of which he'd raised, initially, toward the den from the silence of the study before launching into the sermon on forgiveness.

"Seventy times seven," Vince said aloud, reflecting on the Bible text assigned for the Sunday of Labor Day weekend. "Attendance will be down, fewer people for me to explain the insanity of Jesus's words to a rightly incredulous Peter."

Vince paused at the keyboard, stroked his chin, and typed, "And after all these years of marriage, Molly has come close to moronically maxing out even that monstrous and unmentionably maddening metric."

The pastor laughed softly before pressing the backspace key with his right middle finger. "I can't say that."

Even with the distraction of a new laptop (whose camera portal, Vince realized, remained untaped), the pastor hardly noticed time passing during the previous hour of typing.

He looked at the clock on the far wall of the study and realized he'd have to grab a quick bite and head off to the hospital. The pastor also realized, wistfully, that during normal and recent Friday mornings, he'd still have a few minutes left to hear Mary's wise and reassuring counsel.

Before clicking through four annoying instruction windows and shutting down the new laptop, Vince paused and whispered, "Are you there?"

While staring at the screen, Vince heard the wall clock tick for several seconds. He asked, "Were you ever there?"

The pastor watched the sign-off icons appear, then vanish. He glanced at the clock until the two hands joined in northward symmetry.

"Thanks," he said, leaving his study, "regardless."

Vince walked down the carpeted hallway to the kitchen where Molly held up a sandwich and said, "For you, to go."

She smiled at her husband and handed him his car keys from the row of hooks beside the refrigerator, turning up the volume of a Beatles CD she'd kept on low while Vince was writing.

She hugged her husband. They prayed together at the back door for Lowell and Wilma. Vince included the Chary family in the short prayer.

Molly stood in the carport, watched her husband drive toward the hospital, and listened to the music through the screen door.

"Speaking words of wisdom," sang Paul McCartney. "Let it be."

7

Learning to Love the Weird Parts of the Bible

Make me to know your ways, O Lord; teach me your paths. Lead me in your truth, and teach me, for you are the God of my salvation; for you I wait all day long.

—Psalm 25:4–5

Lord, let me know my end, and what is the measure of my days; let me know how fleeting my life is. . . . For I am your passing guest, an alien, like all my forebears.

—Psalm 39:4, 12

I spent some time before writing "Virginal Laptop" thinking about the last name of the pastor who has a strange cyberencounter with one of the Bible's most famous characters. "Chary," according to the dictionary, describes someone, like me, who is "cautiously or suspiciously reluctant to do something." Pastor Vince is a bit of a control freak, wary of unseen forces that might hijack or impound his carefully worded sermons. To discover that the words you are presently reading are also written on an ancient laptop (never once connected to the internet) tells you all you need to know about my own suspicions and reserved reluctance. My online bank account—accessed through my wife's desktop Apple—is down this morning, with other bank accounts malfunctioning across the nation. Visions of cybercriminality swim through my imagination in tandem with a smug satisfaction that no one can perversely penetrate this particular screen now staring back at me.

Vince loves the Bible and its marvelous stories, but with limits. He wonders about their authenticity and occasional abandonment of common sense. As do I, at times.

At dawn on a recent Tuesday, my wife and I were reading aloud (our morning habit) the account of Saint

Paul's bold testimony in the synagogue in Antioch of Pisidia (Acts 13:13–41). Paul is reminding his Jewish listeners of familiar Bible history and describes a God who for forty years "put up with [the Israelites] in the wilderness" (13:18). A footnote alongside the verb in that quotation led us to these curious words: "Other ancient authorities read *cared for*." Those are two startlingly different choices! "Put up with" versus "cared for." Which is it? God is capable of both divine stances, to be sure, but a careful reader desires clarity. Further investigation that morning led to an annotation that explained the division in translation—in the story's original Greek, the difference in the two verbs consists of a single Greek letter.[1] I find this sort of thing fascinating but also a bit maddening. Friends of mine who wonder about the Bible's reliability are usually not comforted by such curiosities.

Couple this (somewhat regular) literary division in the scholarly ranks with occasional confusion concerning authorship. Does it matter that Saint Paul may not have written all the letters attributed to him? Is it troubling that the Gospel of Luke could have been penned by someone other than a beloved physician bearing the same name? For some, this may initially be something of a deal-breaker. Andrew Hudgins, one of my favorite American poets, recalls the dismay he felt as a young boy upon learning the truth about a beloved mystery

---

1. A short commercial: if you plan to begin any sort of serious Bible reading, consider investing in a version that includes helpful verse annotations written by trusted scholars.

series: "I can still summon, though weakly through the decades, the dismay I felt when I discovered that F. W. Dixon was not really the author of the Hardy Boys books but a pseudonym for many different writers working to a formula. I felt that some tacit agreement had been violated, some faith betrayed. I'd trusted F. W. Dixon, merged my nervous system with his sentences and stories until I was oblivious to the world outside them, and then I found out he didn't exist. O cruel and faithless F. W. Dixon!"[2]

Pseudonymous biblical authorship, though quite common as various books of the Bible came into existence, can also be a troubling discovery for anyone considering (or reconsidering) life in a church community and the stories read and preached upon each Sunday. "This is the Holy Bible!" a friend confided. "Why can't a church making such outlandish claims about God get its act together?"

One of the things I tried to convey in my short story, "Virginal Laptop," is that even pastors—their lives devoted to leading a community shaped by miraculous tales from the past—are flawed and fallible servants who are nonetheless surprised by the revelatory nature of odd stories that lead in rich and inexhaustible directions. This, too, is the Bible's promise for any serious reader. Like Bastian in Michael Ende's marvelous young adult novel, *The Neverending Story*, the careful reader is drawn into a narrative alive with possibility. Bastian

2. Andrew Hudgins, *The Glass Anvil* (Ann Arbor: University of Michigan Press, 1997), 5.

suddenly realizes that he's not only reading a book; he's become part of the book, and the narrative cannot proceed without him. The Bible's ultimate authority rests in its inherent ability to lead the church in directions that are unpredictable, risky, and life-shaping. Vince Chary, Mr. Predictable, discovers that the stories he's been steeped in all these years do indeed speak to him beyond the actual pages of Holy Scripture, which invite him to try something new.

Pastor Chary's vigilant firewall, a laudable attempt to control his interpretive experience, is still delightfully porous regardless of his attempts to be in charge of the process. Part of the Bible's historical appeal is its ability to penetrate human defenses and shape lives. Martin Luther once said the Bible is a "living word," not stagnant. It pulls a reader or listener into the story, penetrating even the most stunted imagination. Just as Walter Cronkite used to say in his old TV show (1953–1957), the Bible attempts to function similarly: "You Are There." Learning to love the very oddness of the Bible—filled with peculiar, open-ended proclivities—is an important part of my own journey in becoming a Christian, still on the way. These old stories are part of God's design in leading a careful reader to truth. And part of their wisdom is that such truth is not instantly attainable. On such truth, any of us can "wait all day long" (Ps. 25:5), or delightfully longer. "Remember the long way," said God to people who'd wandered far and wide in a wilderness (Deut. 8:2). The Bible's thickness and density is intentional.

I am often drawn to the pages of the Bible because it's just downright and colorfully weird. Its stories (per-

CHAPTER 7

haps especially the weird ones) make me think and slow down—way down, something of a gift in a culture that sells instant access to practically everything. In Kevin Smith's rather ribald movie, *Dogma*, Jesus is depicted as the Buddy Christ in a new church campaign known as "Catholicism Wow!"—a deity we can know chummily, like throwing an arm around the shoulder of an old friend.

The Bible, conversely, refuses to remove God's holy, mysterious, sublime, and, yes, strange and evasive nature. There is nothing easy about a serious encounter with its pages. Truth in the Bible is revealed slowly over distilled time with determined patience rather than with a spigot of all-at-once insight. The Bible's challenging stories often, therefore, mirror the real challenge of humans attempting to commune with God, creator of the universe. Philip Yancey writes, "God is infinite, intangible, and invisible . . . we humans have little sympathy for the problems that must confront a Being who desires to relate to us. Baron von Hugel drew the analogy of a man's relations with a dog. The parallel was generous to us. An infinite God relating to human beings presents far more of a challenge than a man relating to his dog—perhaps a man relating to a wood tick is a closer analogy. Communication between such unequal creatures will inevitably cause confusion and disappointment on both sides."[3]

So, why even bother with the Bible? Its stories are often fantastical. Its meaning is regularly layered and

3. Philip Yancey, *Reaching for the Invisible God* (Grand Rapids: Zondervan, 2000), 109.

densely packaged. Its map to truth is often peppered with metaphor, double entendres, misdirection, and surprise. Why is the Bible littered with so many confusing twists and turns? Wouldn't instant clarity and unmistakable revelation result in more converts?

The Bible is not "holy" because that highlighted word appears on its thick, leather-bound spine. I've always thought our national penchant to swear on a Bible in a court of law before telling "the truth, the whole truth, and so on" opens the book to perceived magical propensities (through simple proximity of touch) that the Bible itself never claims.

The Bible is "holy" because it shapes with slow percolation a holy people. It is *meant* to be challenging and difficult because following Jesus and his teachings in your own community will be no walk in the park. A true encounter with the Bible is full of depth with plenty of head scratching, shaping both head and heart. "Put out into the deep water," says Jesus to early would-be disciples, "and let down your nets for a catch" (Luke 5:4).

Jesus does not invite his church into the shallows where there is often a lot of noise. A life of following Jesus will reflect theological depth. Too many Christians splash around in the shallow end of the pool, resulting in lives about as deep as a pizza pan, easily lampooned and understandably rejected by any thinking person. The Bible cannot be skimmed or mined periodically for quick and instant truth. An encounter with its pages will require time and lifelong attention.

The Bible seeks to shape people with deep wisdom worth digging and diving for, far below the surface, leading the church "to maturity, to the measure of the full stature of Christ" (Eph. 4:13). If you're befuddled by the Bible in your initial forays into its pages, take heart. You're on the right track. Its stories—including the odd miracle stories we've been examining—are seeking to change how you walk through this world, heralding a new way of perceiving where we've come from and where we are going.

*

In *The Last Battle*, C. S. Lewis's final book in his famous Narnia series featuring a cast of characters engaged in the long fight between good and evil, there is an exchange between Lucy and her oldest Narnian friend, the Faun Tumnus. They are standing in a high garden, looking out over all of Narnia.

> But when you looked down you found that this hill was much higher than you had thought: it sank down with shining cliffs, thousands of feet below them and trees in that lower world looked no bigger than grains of sea salt. Then [Lucy] turned inward again and stood with her back to the wall and looked at the garden.
> "I see," she said at last, thoughtfully. "I see now. This garden . . . is far bigger inside than it was outside."
> "Of course, Daughter of Eve," said the Faun. "The further up and further in you go, the bigger everything gets. The inside is larger than the outside."[4]

4. C. S. Lewis, *The Last Battle* (New York: Collier Books, 1956), 179–80.

The miracle stories of the Bible, admittedly befuddling and confusing upon first (or thirtieth) encounter, seek to knock us off-kilter. They herald the dawn of a new world initiated by the grace and teachings of Christ. They seek to widen our view of who might be included. They attempt to widen our spiritual imaginations and reveal the deep and wide territory within any human soul. The stories invite us into the promise of this new world that has been initiated in Christ and is also not yet here in its fullness.

Jesus is both with us and ahead of us. He is the light revealed in these strange tales, slowly shaping a new narrative for our present days, "passing guests" (Ps. 39:12) heading toward a garden of justice and peace far larger than anything we can now see.

Recommended Readings

Beck, Richard. *Reviving Old Scratch: Demons and the Devil for Doubters and the Disenchanted*. Minneapolis: Fortress, 2016.

Crews, Harry. *A Childhood: The Biography of a Place*. New York: Penguin Books, 1978.

DeVries, Peter. *The Blood of the Lamb*. New York: Penguin Books, 1961.

DeYoung, Rebecca Konyndyk. *Glittering Vices: A New Look at the Seven Deadly Sins and Their Remedies*. 2nd ed. Grand Rapids: Brazos, 2020.

Dillard, Annie. *Pilgrim at Tinker Creek*. New York: Bantam Books, 1974.

Doyle, Brian. *One Long River of Song*. New York: Little, Brown, 2019.

Haskell, David George. *The Forest Unseen: A Year's Watch in Nature*. New York: Viking, 2012.

Honeycutt, Frank G. *Death by Baptism: Sacramental Liberation in a Culture of Fear*. Minneapolis: Fortress, 2021.

——. *Marry a Pregnant Virgin: Unusual Bible Stories for New and Curious Christians*. Minneapolis: Augsburg Books, 2008.

Keener, Craig S. *Miracles Today: The Supernatural Work of God in the Modern World*. Grand Rapids: Baker Academic, 2021.

Lamott, Anne. *Help, Thanks, Wow: The Three Essential Prayers*. New York: Riverhead Books, 2012.

Lewis, C. S. *The Screwtape Letters*. New York: Bantam Books, 1982.

Raymo, Chet. *Honey from Stone: A Naturalist's Search for God*. New York: Dodd, Mead, 1987.

Robertson, James. *The Testament of Gideon Mack*. New York: Viking, 2007.

Silver, Anna Krugovoy. *Saint Agnostica*. Baton Rouge: Louisiana State University Press, 2021.

Taylor, Barbara Brown. *When God Is Silent*. Boston: Cowley, 1998.

Willimon, William H. *Why Jesus?* Nashville: Abingdon, 2010.

Yancey, Philip. *Reaching for the Invisible God: What Can We Expect to Find?* Grand Rapids: Zondervan, 2000.

Index of Subjects

Index of Scripture